DIARY
of a
Frenchman

François Lambert Bourneuf's Adventures from France to Acadia
1787-1871

Edited and translated by
J. ALPHONSE DEVEAU

NIMBUS PUBLISHING LIMITED

Nimbus Publishing Limited
P.O. Box 9301, Station A
Halifax, Nova Scotia
B3K 5N5

Design: Jay Rutherford, Rutherford/Owen, Halifax
Cover illustration and illustrations p. 12, 23, 49, 53, 70, and 100:
Elizabeth Owen, Rutherford/Owen, Halifax
Map illustrations p. xii, 34: A. Martin Thibodeau

Photo credits: p. vi, Centre d'Etudes Acadiennes, Université de Moncton;
p. viii, 110, and 111, Benoit Comeau; p. ix and 89, Harold Robicheau;
p. 5, François Marette; p. 18, 42, and 57, Nova Scotia Museum; p. 81,
Mrs. Delisle Comeau; p. 83, 86, 102, and 104, Centre Acadien, Université
Sainte-Anne; and p. 112, the Reverend Maurice LeBlanc.

Canadian Cataloguing in Publication Data

Bourneuf, François Lambert, 1787-1871.

Diary of a Frenchman
ISBN 0-921054-42-7
1. Bourneuf, François Lambert, 1787-1871—Diaries.
2. Acadians—Nova Scotia—diaries.
3. Nova Scotia—History—19th century—Biography.
I. Deveau, J. Alphonse, 1917-
II. Title
FC2322.1.B68A3 1990 971.6'02'092 C90-097541-5
F1038.B68A3 1990

Printed and bound in Canada

Contents

Acknowledgements

I am deeply grateful to François Marette, of Domfront, France, for information on the Burnouf family of Regnéville, on naval warfare in the nineteenth century, and on the geography and the history of the regions of France and its colonies. Without his help and involvement, this work would not have been possible.

I am also grateful to Mr. and Mrs. Benoit Comeau for information concerning the descendants of François Lambert Bourneuf and for photographs of members of the family. My appreciation goes as well to Harold Robicheau and Marc Graff, who offered photographs, and to the Centre Acadien, Université Sainte-Anne, for the use of its facilities and photographs. I am also grateful to Lou Collins, Lois Kernaghan, and my cousin Gerald Belliveau, all of Halifax, for their research on Melville Island. Ronald LeBlanc, archivist at the Centre d'Etudes Acadiennes, Université de Moncton, deserves heartfelt thanks for allowing me to use and publish the documents of François Lambert Bourneuf.

J. Alphonse Deveau

Introduction

Although the manuscript left by François
Lambert Bourneuf is often referred to as a
"diary," it is really an autobiography. A diary is
a day-by-day account of a person's life; this is not.

Bourneuf started to write his autobiography in
1859, when he was seventy-one years old. He takes
the reader back to his childhood, in France, and
describes bourgeois life in Regnéville, Normandy,
and his early education. (In France, the family
name was spelled "Burnouf"; in Nova Scotia,
however, it has always been spelled "Bourneuf."
Accordingly, both spellings are used in this book
where appropriate.) Subsequently, he became a
sailor aboard a French frigate, was captured by
the British in 1809, and was incarcerated in
Melville Prison, on the North West Arm in
Halifax.

Bourneuf describes prison conditions in minute
detail, offering a glimpse at Halifax society as
well. His escapes from work crews at Truro, about
fifty miles north of Halifax, and at Prospect,
south of the city, make exciting reading, as does

his odyssey to the French Shore. He eventually settled on St. Mary's Bay, where he became a prosperous businessman, shipbuilder, and member of the Nova Scotia Legislative Assembly from 1843 to 1859.

Bourneuf wrote his autobiography in scribblers that were eight inches by twelve inches. He filled columns taking up half of each page, so it appears that he intended to have his manuscript translated, or rewritten by someone else.

I do not know what happened to Bourneuf's autobiography between the time of its writing and 1891, when the three scribblers came into the possession of Placide Gaudet, Acadian genealogist and historian and part-time editor of the Weymouth newspaper L'Evangéline. *The first two are now in the Placide Gaudet Collection at the Centre d'Etudes Acadiennes, Université de Moncton, New Brunswick. The whereabouts of the third scribbler are unknown. Placide Gaudet published an edited version of the third scribbler in* L'Evangéline *between December 1891 and June 1892, but the scribbler has disappeared from the collection at the Centre d'Etudes Acadiennes. In a letter in the same collection, Gaudet writes that the first scribbler was in the hands of Captain Leander Pothier, of Grosses Coques, on St. Mary's Bay. Gaudet, therefore, must have obtained it at a later date, as it is in the Moncton collection.*

On January 14, 1947, J. Willie Comeau, an MLA and a great-grandson of François Lambert Bourneuf, gave a talk on his illustrious forebear to members of the Nova Scotia Historical Society. He presented a translation of part of the third scribbler, as it had appeared in L'Evangéline; *this translation is now in the Public Archives of Nova Scotia. The* L'Evangéline *version is also in Volume 27 of the* Nova Scotia Historical Society Collections.

This book is an annotated translation of the first two scribblers and the excerpts in L'Evangéline. *I have tried to maintain the style and vocabulary of the author as much as possible.*

J.A.D.

François Lambert Bourneuf, MLA

Prologue

Bourneuf began writing his autobiography in the spring of 1859, while he was in Halifax for a sitting of the Nova Scotia Legislative Assembly. He had represented the Township of Digby County since 1843. Up to 1859, Digby County comprised three electoral ridings: the Township of Clare, represented by Mathurin Robichaud,[1] Digby Town and Hillsborough, represented by John Chipman Wade,[2] and the Township of Digby County, which included the area from Weymouth to Digby Town, Digby Neck, and Long and Brier islands.

In November 1855, Bourneuf suffered severe financial losses. As a result, he had to declare bankruptcy, which affected his health to the point of a nervous breakdown. He believed that he was not responsible for his financial misfortune, so he decided to write his autobiography to redeem himself in the eyes of his constituents. Indeed, the work begins with his asking for support in the provincial election that took place in the fall of 1859.

1. Born in Meteghan in 1810, Mathurin Robichaud represented the Township of Clare from 1855 to 1859 and Digby County from 1859 to 1867. During that time, he was a "Liberal-Conservative." A merchant and justice of the peace, he became the lighthouse keeper at Cape St. Mary's after he resigned from office. He died in 1892 and is buried in the Salmon River cemetery.

2. John Chipman Wade was born in Granville in 1817. He practised law in Digby and became a Liberal MLA in 1851, serving as Speaker of the Legislative Assembly from 1864 to 1867. He died in 1892.

The central issue of the day was the rising tension between Catholics and Protestants. The Catholic Liberal members of the Legislative Assembly had crossed the floor in protest against Joseph Howe's attack on Catholicism, and this action brought about the downfall of the Liberal government.

3. *Colin Campbell, Jr., was born in Shelburne in 1822, son of Colin Campbell, Sr., who was MLA for the Township of Shelburne from 1793 to 1818. Colin Campbell, Jr., was a pioneer shipbuilder, lumber exporter, and merchant. He was a member of the Executive Council, or provincial cabinet, from 1860 to 1863 and again from 1875 to 1878. He died suddenly in 1881 and was buried in Weymouth.*

When Bourneuf started to write his memoirs, the election had not yet been called, and although he does not mention it, the township system of representation had been abolished during the session. Thereafter, Digby County became a triple riding. Each voter—at the time, each male property owner—was allowed to vote for three candidates. The three candidates garnering the most votes were elected regardless of party affiliation. Bourneuf was not re-elected in 1859; Mathurin Robichaud, John Chipman Wade, and Colin Campbell, Jr.,[3] of Weymouth, were sent to the legislature.

To the electors of Digby County:

YOU HAVE HONOURED ME by electing me in the last four elections, in which I was a candidate for the Legislative Assembly at Halifax. In the last election, you elected me with a majority of 240 votes over my closest opponent.

I have presented to the Assembly all of the petitions and the requests that you have asked me to make, either in writing or verbally. If I have not succeeded in each and every petition and request that I presented to the Assembly, I hope I have not done anything to displease you. If I did so, I ask your pardon.

I ask once more for your support in the coming general election. If you honour me again by re-electing me, I will do better than I have in the past. During the past sixteen years that I have represented you, I have learned a lot; I did not have that experience when I was first elected.

My business[4] has suffered great losses, and some may believe that it is my fault. I am going to prove in this work, which I will put before you, that I am not responsible for the misfortune that has befallen me. People have cheated me and stolen from me, and I hope that you will understand what I went through and that you will not blame me. I may have lost my property, but I have not lost my honour. It is better to have credit and a good name rather than property.

4. *Bourneuf's business interests comprised shipbuilding at Grosses Coques, shipping, stores at Grosses Coques and Belliveau Cove, and large holdings of timberland.*

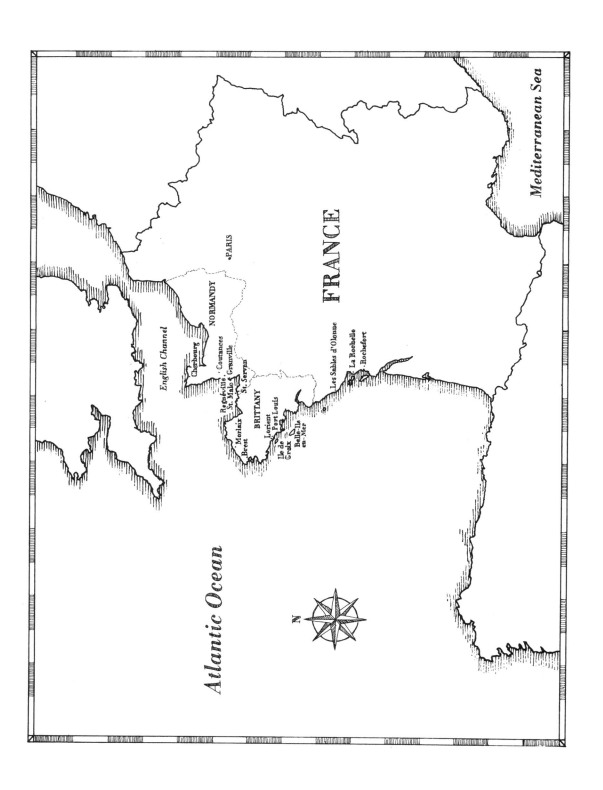

Mediterranean Sea

English Channel

•PARIS

NORMANDY

FRANCE

Cherbourg

Coutances
Granville
St. Malo
St. Servan

Roscoff
Morlaix
BRETAGNE BRITTANY
Brest
Lorient
Port Louis
Ile de
Groix
Belle-Ile
en-Mer

Les Sables d'Olonne
La Rochelle
Rochefort

Atlantic Ocean

N

The Burnouf Family in France

*T*he first two pages of François Lambert
Bourneuf's autobiography are missing, but
one can easily assume that they included information on his ancestors, for the third page opens
with comments concerning his grandfather's
brother, a surgeon in Coutances, France.

*Given the livelihood and status of some members
of the Burnouf family, it appears that they
belonged to the bourgeois class, as it was known
before the French Revolution.*

*Bourneuf's paternal ancestry can be traced back
to the first half of the seventeenth century. Nicolas
Burnouf, a lawyer of the parish of St. Nicolas, in
Coutances, married Michelle de Moyne in 1656.
They had two sons—Jean, born about 1670, and
Henri—and two daughters—Anne, born on
August 25, 1677, and Françoise, who died before
age one. Jean, Sieur de la Fonnière, was an
officer in the French Admiralty. He married
Marguerite Barben on January 13, 1697, and he*

died before 1744. Henri married Marguerite Aubuisson, and Anne married Noel le Sueur, a bourgeois merchant.

Henri and Marguerite had ten children. Of these, only three had descendants: François, Bourneuf's grandfather, born in 1705; Pierre, the surgeon in Coutances, born in 1697; and Charles Lô, born in 1695 and later married to Marguerite Hommeril. François married Marie Le Nepveu on July 29, 1742, and they had seven sons and one daughter, Anne, born in 1746 and married on January 30, 1771, to Nicolas Novince, of Regnéville. Of the seven sons, five were seamen, and one was a governor in the West Indies. Another, Pierre Lô, died at a young age.

Although Bourneuf says that his father, François-Louis, was the youngest of the family, this is not the case. Jean-Charles Lô, born in 1757, was the youngest; according to the parish registers of Regnéville, Grimonville, and Orville, France, François-Louis was born in 1754. As the sixth son of the family, François-Louis did not inherit much of his father's estate. Under the Ancien Régime, the droit d'aînesse *prevailed; that is, the oldest son inherited the largest share of family property, if not all of it. Nevertheless, François-Louis was not poor by any means: he owned four houses in and around Regnéville.*

An examination of the family tree shows that the Burnouf family was relatively well off and was certainly bourgeois. At least two members were doctors,[1] two were officials in the French Admiralty, two were lawyers, and two were merchants. The fact that three of the surgeon Pierre Burnouf's daughters married wealthy husbands indicates that they were able to contribute substantial dowries.

Bourneuf offers further details about his ancestry. He begins with a description of his great-uncle Pierre.

1. *In the Ancien Régime, medicine was considered one of the noble professions.*

HIS THREE DAUGHTERS married gentlemen of means, and the old man was left alone. He was much wealthier than my grandfather, and I believe that he had acquired his wealth through his medical practice. Unfortunately, he had become blind. Even though he could not see, he continued to attend to the sick. One of my brothers broke his arm, and my great-uncle put it back into place.

In his old age, Pierre decided to remarry. He married a young girl and gave her part of his property, which greatly displeased his children.

One of his grandsons[2] is a member of the Academy in Paris. I read in a newspaper that he was a candidate in a national election. However, I never learned whether he won or lost. The Count of Baruel,[3] secretary of Lord Forland, told me that he knew him.

My grandfather and my grandmother died before I was born. They had six sons and one daughter. One son, Charles, was Governor of St. Lucia [the West Indies] before the British captured it. During one of his voyages, my father visited Charles. Consequently, Charles left his property to him.

My father, François-Louis, was the youngest of his family and was raised by his sister. He was not so fortunate as his brothers, for he was young when his father and mother died. When he came of age, he learned carpentry, then went to sea.

In peacetime, he was a mate on the ships that went fishing on the Grand Banks of Newfoundland, and in wartime, he was a master carpenter in the French Navy. Since the French Revolution, all sailors who are between the ages of sixteen and fifty-nine and who are physically able must serve in the Navy during wartime. My father served from the beginning of the Revolution[4] to 1804.

In 1802, during a brief armistice[5] between France and England, he left Lorient, Brittany. Along with

2. Eugène Burnouf, a noted French authority on Oriental languages and cultures, was a member of the Académie des Inscriptions et Belles Lettres, which specializes in history and archaeology.

3. Bourneuf probably knew the Count of Baruel through his business connections in France and Great Britain.

4. The French Revolution began in 1789. Bourneuf's father actually entered the Navy in 1792, the year the French government introduced compulsory military service.

5. The Treaty of Amiens was signed on March 27, 1802. The armistice lasted until May 16, 1803, when England declared war on France.

Joseph Bonaparte,[6] he sailed to Martinique [the West Indies] aboard a brig named *L'Epervier*. While on Martinique, war was declared. Joseph Bonaparte, afraid of being captured by the British, took passage on an American ship and went to Baltimore. There, he married a Miss Patterson. Then he left her and returned to France. She tried to join him but landed in England, where she gave birth to a son. The Emperor refused to recognize the son as legitimate, but the Holy Father did. At present, the son[7] is in Paris and is the highest-ranking prince of the Empire. Miss Patterson has since remarried.

I will now return to my father, on Martinique. He sailed for France on the *L'Epervier*, but it was captured by a British frigate.[8] En route, the frigate came across a British brig that had lost its rudder. As my father was a ship's carpenter, he was ordered to make a new rudder. The British captain thought my father was a Swede,[9] so he gave him a good sum of money and put him on a parliamentary ship[10] sailing for Morlaix, France.

After that, my father did not sail on warships. He drafted his will, dividing his property among me and my brothers. He then wrote to me in St. Mary's Bay, telling me about the property. As I did not need it, I replied that he could have it and dispose of it as he wished. By the time my letter arrived in France, however, my father,

6. *Jérôme Bonaparte, not Joseph, accompanied Bourneuf's father to Martinique. Jérôme, a lieutenant in the French Navy, married Elizabeth Patterson, daughter of a banker. (Joseph Bonaparte, oldest brother of Napoleon I, was made King of Naples and then King of Spain.) Napoleon annulled the marriage, and at his request, Jérôme married Catherine, Princess of Würtemberg.*

7. *Elizabeth Patterson and her son, Jérôme Bonaparte, Jr., returned to the United States. He became the father of Charles Joseph Bonaparte, Secretary of the Navy in 1905 and Attorney General from 1906 to 1909. It was Jérôme Bonaparte's son with Catherine of Würtemberg that was the pretender to the throne of Napoleon.*

8. *At this time, a frigate was a fully rigged three-masted vessel that carried between thirty and fifty guns on one deck. L'Epervier (front) was captured by a British frigate*

9. *Sweden was a neutral country.*

10. *During wartime, "parliamentary" ships sailed between enemy nations to exchange prisoners or diplomats.*

at age sixty-six, was dead. I returned to France in
1846[11] and gave my inheritance to my sister.

My mother, Françoise Michelle Enole, was a tall
woman. She had nine children:[12] eight boys and one
girl, Jeanne Françoise, who was the oldest. The oldest
and youngest boys died young, and the third child,
Charles, died in Ile de France. I was the fourth, and
after me, my mother had twins, Pierre and Jean, and
three more boys. The youngest child was not
baptized.[13]

As my father was at sea, my mother was left alone to
care for the children. She also looked after the household and the farm, which was located a league from
home. She hired men to plough the land, cut the hay,
and stook and thresh the wheat. She had to see to
everything inside and outside the house. She washed
our clothes, milked two cows, and tended twenty sheep.
She sometimes hired girls to help her: during wartime,
there were only old and lame men and young boys left
at home. My father did send her plenty of money, for he
made good wages. He earned 120 francs[14] per month,
plus 40 francs' allowance for his board, and a ration
above that.

You can imagine, however, that my mother did not
have an easy life. She died suddenly at age forty-nine,
when I was twelve years old. My sister brought me up,
so that is why I gave her all my inheritance.

All my brothers are dead now. Charles, as I said,
died in Ile de France; Jean, also in France; and Julien,
aboard a warship at Martinique. Jean joined me in St.
Mary's Bay, while Pierre took care of my father in his
old age. During this time, Pierre married a woman with
no savings. She had owned an inn and a bakery and had
gone deeply into debt, so my father had to sell part of
his property. This also impoverished Pierre. He went
fishing off Newfoundland in a French vessel and died
there of grief.

---

11. *This was the only time
that Bourneuf
returned to France
after settling on St.
Mary's Bay. He had
left home in 1809 on a
frigate, and his family
had given him up for
dead.*

12. *According to the
Regnéville parish
register, the birthdates
of François-Louis
Burnouf and Françoise
Michelle Enole's
children are as follows:
Jeanne Françoise, May
25, 1784; François
Lambert, May 30,
1785 (died in 1786);
Charles François,
August 24, 1786;
François Lambert,
November 19, 1787;
Pierre and Jean,
September 28, 1789;
Julien, December 4,
1790; Jean-Baptiste,
1791. One other died
at birth, in 1793.*

13. *Baptism was an
important rite.
According to Roman
Catholic belief, if a
child died before being
baptized, his soul would
not go to heaven, but
would remain in limbo
forever.*

14. *The franc was worth
about twenty cents
Canadian.*

Schooling

Surprisingly, Bourneuf does not talk about his early childhood. This would have been during the worst part of the French Revolution, from 1792 to 1799. Either he does not remember anything about it, or the family was not affected, except for his father, who was serving in the Navy. He does not mention whether anyone in his father's family was imprisoned, exiled, or executed. Perhaps the Burnoufs supported the French Republic?

Instead, Bourneuf begins with his schooling. He briefly attended a day public school and later completed his elementary education at a state boarding school. In France, a public-school system was introduced during the early part of the Revolution. There were private institutions as well, run by religious orders of priests, brothers, or nuns; children often lived at these schools, and parents paid room and board and tuition. Many of the religious orders immigrated to Canada, such as the Eudist Fathers, who became established at Church Point, Nova Scotia, and the Sisters of

Notre Dame, who had a convent at Chéticamp, Cape Breton.

Bourneuf received much of his schooling, however, from Father Pierre Blondel, the pastor in Regnéville. From 1792 to 1804, when Napoleon I became Emperor, the Catholic clergy in France suffered a great deal. The clergy had to swear allegiance to the Republic and to sever all ties with the Pope by accepting a civil constitution that made the Church subservient to the State; the pastors and curates who refused had to leave the country. (One such clergyman was Father Jean-Mandé Sigogne, who welcomed Bourneuf when he arrived in St. Mary's Bay.) Because Blondel remained in his parish throughout the Revolution, one can surmise that he accepted the Civil Constitution.

NOW I WILL TELL YOU how I got my education. My mother sent me to a public school when I was very young, and that is where I learned my letters.

At that time, my father owned four houses, and we lived in the largest. Built of cut stone, our home was very beautiful. Three gardens surrounded the house, and two gates, locked every night, allowed access to these gardens, one of which was quite large and had a vegetable patch, as well as fruit trees. The gardens were enclosed by eight-foot-high walls built of lime and stone. Fruit trees of every kind—apple, pear, plum, and apricot—lined one wall, which was also the wall of the cemetery.

Our old pastor often came to our house, where he wrote the correspondence of my mother to my father.[1] He took a liking to me. I served his mass every morning, so, to reward me, he taught me to read and write.

1. *Bourneuf's father was serving in the Navy.*

At his home, he left work for me in a large room that was under his bedroom. Because he slept until eight or nine o'clock every morning, I went early to do the exercises. When he got up, I could hear him making his bed and sweeping his room. When he was finished sweeping, I climbed the stairs and knocked on his door. Sometimes, he said, in a voice like a farmer's, "Open." Other times, he said, "One moment." When he was ready, he said, "Open." Then I entered, and I always found him wearing a long white dressing robe.

He made me sit down at his table, and he examined my exercises. After he had made corrections, he made me stand up to read. When I did not read as well as he wanted, he cried aloud, "God, give me patience." God forgot sometimes, however, and the pastor would strike me between my shoulder blades with his fist and send me sprawling on the floor. When he picked me up, I was crying and could not see well enough to read any more. He would send me home, and I would tell my dear mother, "The old fatso beat me again. I will not go to his school any more. He is too bad." My mother would say, "My dear little boy, you must return; he will not beat you again." But this happened more than twenty times. The pastor was about four and a half feet tall and weighed about three hundred pounds. When he put his weight behind his blows, think what it did to me, a mere boy. He did not hit me because he was bad, however: it was God who did not provide him with what he needed, patience.

The old pastor's name was Pierre Blondel. He was born in Coutances, two leagues[2] from Regnéville. He loved me like a son: he gave me many gifts and invited me to eat at his table many times. He had a maid who cooked for him and did the household chores, as well as many others, including milking the cows and tending the garden. She was called Louison, but I do not know her family name. When the pastor went visiting, he brought her along. Sometimes they took me, too.

The good pastor never ate breakfast. For his dinner, he always had something good to eat, and drank a three-quart carafe of cider that was so strong that it brought tears to my eyes. Sometimes he drank two bottles of wine that Louison had made.

The maid was as big as the pastor, but she was taller. A good-looking woman, she had been sought after in marriage many times, but she did not want to leave the pastor. She had the keys to everything and did not seem like his maid: she and the pastor lived more like brother and sister.

They lived in a large glebe house[3] that had more than twenty rooms. They had a barn that had been built when the clergy still received tithes,[4] and they had the loveliest garden in the world.

The garden was surrounded by ten-foot-high walls with gateways made of cut stone. It was large and had pretty pathways along vegetable squares that were arranged in perfect order. There were all kinds of fruit

2. One league equals three miles.

3. The "glebe house" was the residence of the priest. It was usually quite large, for in addition to the priest, it often had to accommodate one or two curates. As well, it had to have rooms for the Bishop and his attendant when they made pastoral visits, and separate quarters for the maid.

4. A "tithe" was a tax for support of the clergy. Generally, it was one tenth of a person's income.

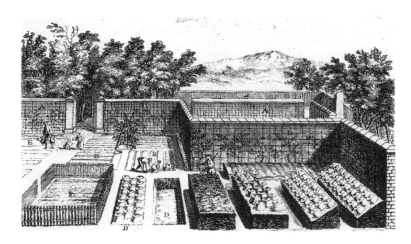

trees grafted with the best fruit, and there were all kinds
of fowl and pigeons and domesticated rabbits.

The pastor and his maid spent their leisure time
working in the garden, and they hired gardeners by the
day to help them. None of them stayed at the glebe
house overnight.

I will tell you how the pastor treated me when we
were in his garden. He spoke softly with a voice as deep
as his belly: "François my boy, come with me." And he
would take me to his garden and say, "Here is a goose-
berry bush. You eat all the gooseberries before going to
another bush. After you have eaten all of them, I will
give you another bush." The good pastor did as he
promised and gave me as much fruit as I wanted.

The pastor and his maid also had an outdoor oven.
The villagers used it to bake their bread, and it was large
enough to hold the bread of three or four families at
once, or more than twenty or thirty loaves weighing
twenty or thirty pounds each.[5]

The oven was used day and night, except on Sundays, so it did not take long to heat. The maid kept a
register so that families knew when it was their turn to
bake bread. In summer, they baked bread every week; in
winter, every two weeks. They brought enough fire-
wood for their baking, and the women helped to keep

5. *Obviously, these weights
are exaggerated.*

Outdoor ovens, made of brick or stone, were about six feet in diameter and were shaped like a beehive. They were divided horizontally into two parts: a lower compartment where the wood was burned to heat the structure, and an upper compartment where the bread was baked. Once the oven was heated to the required temperature, the bread was put in the upper part, and the iron door tightly shut.

6. *Hardwood ashes were used to make lye.*

the oven hot and to put in the loaves of bread. After three hours, the loaves were done and removed from the oven. Then there was always another "company" waiting. For her work, the maid received only the ashes, but she made a lot of money from them, for ashes were in great demand.[6]

In addition to the glebe house, the pastor had four other large houses. His two unmarried sisters, who were quite old, took care of those homes. I delivered many letters to his sisters, and when I did, they always treated me well, giving me candy and fruit while I waited for them to write replies. They were religious sisters, but I do not know which order they belonged to. Whenever I left them, they did not kiss me, as it was not the custom for religious sisters to kiss men or boys. But they were so kind to me that it was worth more than all the kisses.

In 1798, I left the pastor and went to a state boarding school where I remained for one year. During that time, my mother died suddenly. A messenger came for me, and he said that my father had sent for me, but did not know why. I thought right away that somebody at home had died, but I did not believe that it was my mother.

When I was two and a half leagues from home, I started to weep, thinking that some misfortune had befallen my family. Near the house, I heard the church bell toll the dirge, and this deepened my sorrow.

Before I arrived home, a woman ran after me to tell me that my mother had died. I fainted, and when I came to, my family wanted to take me to see my mother. But I did not have the courage, and I did not attend the funeral. I was in such deep sorrow that I could not eat. Not a day passed that I did not weep for her.

I had become so weak that I fainted everywhere—at home and at church. My father did not know what to do with me, so he made me go to sea with one of my uncles, Captain Lambert Burnouf, who was in the coastal trade. That took my mind off my sadness, and I regained my courage. But when I saw the house again, with no mother, the sorrow returned. I wanted to die a hundred times and would have been happy if death had taken me. But I continued to go on voyages with my uncle. Sometimes I was gone for three months, and little by little, I recovered from the death of my mother.

Service in the Emperor's Navy

Napoleon I

1. Brest still is France's main military port on the Atlantic. It was the main port of entry for American troops during World War I and a base for the German Navy during World War II.

Bourneuf now jumps ahead to the Napoleonic Wars and his military service. In 1792, the Republic had established compulsory military service for every able-bodied Frenchman.

Bourneuf himself must have been called up after 1804, for he refers to the "Emperor." Napoleon I took the title Emperor in May of that year and was crowned the following December.

Until the end of his reign in 1814, Napoleon led his country in a war against Britain—and nearly all of Europe. On land, Napoleon's armies invaded Austria, Prussia, Spain, the Kingdom of Naples, Russia, and Turkey. At sea, the struggle was between France and Britain. Bourneuf served on a French frigate, and later, he describes some of the battles. In this chapter, however, he deals mostly with life in the French ports of Brest[1] and Recouvrance.

AFTER GOING TO SEA with my uncle, I sailed for three years with Captain Pierre David. Then I was called to serve His Majesty, the Emperor of the French.

I was given a road ticket, which is like a passport. There were many of us, and we all received three sous[2] a month, with one month's allowance in advance.

We were sent to Brest, seventy leagues from home. Along the way, we could have used vouchers for lodging, but we preferred to pay out of our own pockets: the mayor of a town supplied the vouchers, and sometimes he sent us a league out of our way. If there was no mayor in the town we stopped in, an officer issued the vouchers.

It took ten days to reach Brest, and when we arrived, we reported to the naval office, where the captain assigned us to a destination. We thought we were going to be assigned to one of the vessels in port, but we were sent to barracks in Recouvrance.

The port of Brest is a very deep river. Ships that draw twenty-five feet of water can always remain afloat. The harbour itself is about a quarter of a mile wide, walled with enormous cut stones held together by cement and lead. The river is six or seven miles long, and ships can sail to the end of it. There are basins along the shores where vessels are built and repaired.

On either side of the port is a town: one is Brest, and the other is Recouvrance.[3] They are well protected. At the entrance to the port, and all around, there are fortifications with cannons and mortars that can sink any vessel in their wake.

In the middle of one of the towns, there is a penitentiary that holds more than five hundred convicts, who work in chaingangs. They do the heaviest labour and are only fed coarse bread. Guards of the *chiourme*[4] lead the convicts to the work areas. You must be careful when you go near the prisoners, for they are such thieves and sleight-of-hand experts that they can steal

2. *At this time, the sou was worth one twentieth of a franc, or "half an English penny."*

3. *Recouvrance is now part of the city of Brest.*

4. Chiourme *is French slang for "convict." In France, life for convicts was especially harsh. The heaviest labour consisted of crushing stones with a heavy mall from sunrise to sunset; the crushed rock was used for building roads and for construction. If prisoners disobeyed orders or tried to escape, they faced flogging or the guillotine. French convicts were also sent to the colonies. Before it was sold in 1804 to the United States, Louisiana received prisoners; the infamous penal colony of Devil's Island, off the coast of French Guiana, was established after 1830.*

5. *"Scurvy" is a disease caused by a lack of ascorbic acid or vitamin C. It was once common among sailors who were deprived of fresh fruit and vegetables during long voyages. Instead, they lived on salt beef and hard tack (dry biscuits). On one of his voyages, the Portuguese explorer Vasco da Gama lost 100 of 160 men. In 1795, the British Navy began issuing daily rations of lime juice to prevent*

everything you are carrying: handkerchiefs, money, watches. But some of them are tradesmen who can make the most beautiful objects, especially pieces of jewellery.

When we went to Recouvrance, we learned how to fire cannons and guns, and I was promoted to Corporal. After a month, two frigates arrived from the Arctic Ocean, where they had gone to destroy British whaling ships. They had destroyed many and had captured a ship from Québec that was laden with beaver and seal pelts. A British fleet pursued them, but they escaped by taking refuge in the Rivière des Erdieu.

The frigates had lost many men to scurvy,[5] so their crews had to be replenished. I was one of those chosen to go on board.

First, we had to go to the naval office in Brest. Boats provided this service, and twenty of us—too many—embarked on one. After we sat down, we pushed off, leaving the boatman behind on shore, playing with some companions. When he saw his boat leaving without him, he threw stones at us. Those who saw the stones coming ducked and fell on the others, swamping the boat. Seven men drowned, but I swam like a fish and reached the shore—the first to do so.

A sloop of war took the survivors to the frigates. There were so many passengers in the sloop, however, that we were put in the hold. Some of us were taken to one frigate, and the rest to the other.

As it was winter, I had caught a cold from swimming, and a fever had struck while I was on the sloop. I was placed in the frigate hospital for the night, then the following day, I was taken by cart to a hospital two leagues away.

The good Sisters of Charity ran the hospital, and they were very good to me. I was lying in a bed that had been used by an unclean person, so my clothes were full of lice. I was so weak that I did not notice, but the Sisters did, and they changed my clothes and the bed right away. They took care of me as my own mother would have.

Although they brought me preserves and candies, I went eight days without eating. I could drink only herb tea or a little wine mixed with water. The first thing I ate was a baked apple. After I had eaten it, the fever went away little by little. I was sick for thirty days, and then I regained my health slowly. I was so weak, however, that I could not walk for a long while.

When I recovered, the two frigates received orders to go to St. Malo.[6] I was still weak, but I asked to go aboard the frigate to which I had been assigned. Too frail to carry out my duties, I was left alone to do what I could. In a few days, we left for St. Malo, and we arrived at our destination without difficulty.

At St. Malo, we saw many French ships. I was granted one month's sick leave, but I took two. I then rejoined my frigate, still at St. Malo.

While there, I was assigned to work on the *Cano Major*, which took officers back and forth from the ship to land. The men on the *Cano Major* were well treated and well dressed and much better off than those who remained on board the frigate, named *La Sirène*, which needed repair work. The other frigate, the *Revanche*, was old and finally condemned, but it was replaced by a beautiful new vessel, *L'Italienne*. After a year at St. Malo, we received orders to prepare to sail.

the disease, whose symptoms include anaemia, wounds that do not heal, sore gums and mouth, and loose teeth.

6. *Facing the English Channel, St. Malo is a famous port on the northwest coast of France. Jacques Cartier, for example, set sail from St. Malo.*

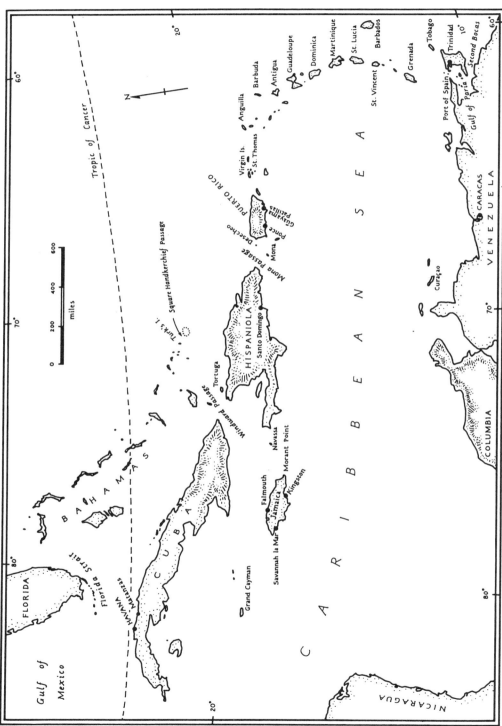

The West Indies

Encounters with the Enemy

In early 1807, the war in Europe was still going in Napoleon's favour. In February, France and Russia fought to a draw at Eylau, in Prussia, but on June 14, Napoleon's armies defeated Russian forces at Friedland. France also defeated Prussia at Jena and Auerstadt; Prussia gave up half of its territory, and Napoleon made his brother Jérôme King of Westphalia.

The same year, Napoleon occupied Portugal, and in 1808, French armies invaded Spain, forcing Ferdinand VII to abdicate. Napoleon's brother Joseph then became King of Spain, with Joachim Murat replacing him as King of Naples.

Britain then invaded Spain, launching the Peninsular War, which lasted for five years. In 1809, Austria declared war on France but was defeated after a four-month campaign.

At sea, Napoleon's forces were not faring so well. At the hands of the British fleet, the French Navy suffered setbacks in Egypt, in the English

Channel, and off the coast of Spain. Britain now threatened French shipping, as well as France's possessions in the West Indies. At this time, France controlled Haiti, Martinique, Guadeloupe, Iles des Saintes, and Marie Galante; Britain had Jamaica, the Bahamas, the Caicos Islands, the Turks Islands, the Virgin Islands, Anguilla, Antigua, Montserrat, Dominica, St. Lucia, St. Vincent, Grenada, Barbados, Trinidad, and Tobago.

Britain and France saw the West Indies as vital possessions: they were principal sources of sugar, rum, and salt; they were important ports of call for merchant fleets in need of supplies; and they were strategic safeguards of their overseas colonies. Given the number of its island possessions, Britain had a decided edge.

Bourneuf sails on La Sirène, *from St. Malo to Martinique. On the return trip, his frigate is surrounded by British warships near Ile de Groix, off the coast of France.*

THE GOVERNMENT NEVER REVEALS the destination of a ship, not even to the commander. The Admiral and the Captain receive a sealed envelope and are told in writing to set their course for a certain longitude and latitude. When they arrive at that point, they open the envelope and find another letter, or despatch, that tells them to go to another longitude and latitude. In that way, they do not know where they are going until they reach their final destination. Only the Minister of the Navy knows the routes of ships.

At St. Malo, our frigate, *La Sirène,* took on troops, cannon powder, bombs, shot, and large mortars. We followed the despatches of the Minister of the Navy, saw the Azores, and finally arrived at Fort Royal, on Martinique, without any incident worthy of mention.

When we entered the *barachois,*[1] the troops and the war supplies were sent ashore, but we remained on board the frigate. After thirty-six hours, we set sail for France.

On the return trip, we captured many enemy ships, though I do not remember the number. We kept one British warship with us for a few days, but it could not maintain our speed, so we burned it. Then we took a large British merchant ship loaded with goods. Three ships shared the cargo, taking only the superior merchandise. The British captain had the invoices, indicating which bales of goods were the most valuable.

A few days later, we captured a British brig loaded with Jamaican rum. This time, two frigates divided the cargo, and afterwards, each sailor received four or five glasses of rum during the day and during each watch at night.

Every sailor had a trunk with his name on it, and every trunk contained its owner's share of the spoils. The trunks were kept in the powder magazine and given to the men on landing in France. Some sailors had a rousing good time with their share. But I sent a dress

1. *The word* barachois *is a common noun that has several meanings. In this instance, it refers to a shelter situated in a harbour.*

2. *Lorient, on the west coast of France, was a German submarine base during World War II. It is still an important French naval base.*

3. *Harbour pilots guided ships through hazardous waters. Once on board, they were entirely responsible for the ship's safety. They had to be familiar with the currents, shoals, and depths of the waters.*

4. *According to official reports, the Battle of Groix took place in March (La Sirène arrived at Ile de Groix on March 22, 1808), with the British squadron consisting of five ships. For further descriptions of the battle, see O. Troude,* Batailles Navales de la France *(Paris, 1868), and Laird Clowes,* The Royal Navy: A History from the Earliest Times to the Present *(London).*

5. *Captain Victor Guy Dupérré was a brilliant French naval officer. He was born in La Rochelle in 1775 and died in 1846. He eventually became Admiral of the French Navy and commanded the squadron that captured Algiers in 1830.*

and many yards of cotton to my sister and all my lady cousins. When I visited them in 1846, they came to see me and expressed their thanks. This touched me deeply and brought back many memories.

We arrived off the coast of France without incident. At Ile de Groix, several leagues from Lorient,[2] the pilots[3] came aboard. We were then becalmed for four or five hours.

At five o'clock in the evening, the watch cried out, "Ships ahoy."

"From what direction are they coming?" the Captain asked. "How many and what kind of ship?"

"They're coming with the wind," the watch replied, "and there are five of them, three-masters at about fifteen leagues."

We were still becalmed, but the British ships had a land breeze, which rises every evening in summer. It was the month of May.[4]

Using his spyglass, the Captain, named Dupérré,[5] saw that there were three ships of the line and two frigates. They were rapidly closing in on us.

Captain Dupérré ordered that all boats be lowered. On a warship, everybody knows what to do, and everybody knows his post. The crews, in their boats, began to tow the frigates out of danger. But the British had a good breeze, and it was getting dark. About ten o'clock, the Captain re-called all the boats. Once on board, the crew manned the battle stations.

One of the enemy ships came so close that the Captain touched the rail with his hand. Then a frigate approached us from the other side. The English commander yelled, "Ho, the little frigate, surrender or I sink you!" Our captain said, "Shit." The firing began.

Captain Dupérré cried through his megaphone: "Load the cannons on both sides. Be careful, sight the ships before firing. Courage, my boys." Then he gave each of us a pint of wine mixed with powder.[6]

The French hoisted three lanterns, instead of flags, in a triangle,[7] and the British hoisted three lanterns in single file. The Captain then had the bright idea to arrange the lanterns in single file. This was done in the twinkling of an eye, and it confused the British: they started fighting among themselves.

Captain Dupérré took the lanterns down and ordered the men to close the portholes.[8] Then we slipped away under the guns of a large fort on Ile de Groix. The British ships continued to fight among themselves for three quarters of an hour, inflicting terrible damage on each other. One ship even had to leave the next day for repairs. Meanwhile, we became grounded and had to throw our cannons overboard.

Our frigate, *La Sirène,* was heavily damaged, and many ships and frigates anchored in the port of Lorient sent small boats to help us. After three days, *La Sirène* was afloat; it took about thirty vessels to tow it into Lorient. Unfortunately, the ship was so badly damaged that it was condemned and refurbished as a pontoon.

During the battle, twenty men had been killed and thirty had been wounded. One man had escaped the skirmish altogether. Before battle, a roll call was taken, as always. One sailor did not answer, so the following

6. *A mixture of wine and powder was often given to men before battle, to calm them.*

7. *Ships of different nations used various light signals to identify themselves. Although Dupérré used three lanterns in a triangle, this was not a configuration of the French Republic.*

8. *The portholes were the openings for the cannons. Dupérré ordered them closed because firing the cannons would have given away* La Sirène's *position. With the lanterns down and the portholes shut, the frigate could slip away to safety.*

9. *Rolling a man down a mountain in a cask full of nails was an extraordinary punishment for the French Navy. Other navies flogged recalcitrant sailors to death. Another drastic and often fatal punishment was keelhauling. The victim was hauled under the keel from one side of the ship to the other.*

day, another roll call was taken. We looked for the missing man and found him lying in the hold. He was brought up on deck, and Captain Dupérré asked him why he had not been present. The man said that he was sick, but the ship's doctor examined him and found nothing wrong. He was not sick: he was scared.

The Captain ordered the ship's carpenters to prepare a cask. They drove nails through it, and all over it. Then he had the cask and the man brought to the top of a high mountain near the port. But before the culprit was put in the cask to roll down the mountain,[9] he died.

God had spared him a martyr's death. And it was a good thing, for he was saved from dishonouring his family. In France, a cowardly man dishonours his family, while a brave man brings honour. If a member of a

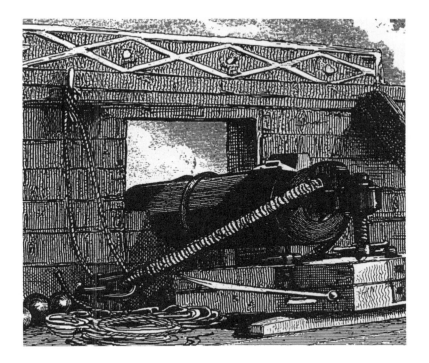

10. *The typical battery of a French frigate was forty-two 36-calibre carronades. The* Furieuse *carried twelve of these, in addition to two 18-calibre cannons. The carronade was named after Carron, the place in Scotland where it was first cast, and was widely used on warships after 1700.*

family is brave, people say the whole family is courageous.

When we arrived at Lorient, we removed the armaments from *La Sirène* and placed them on a barge. At Lorient, we worked in the shipyard for three months. Then we were moved to large barracks. We practised firing guns and cannons on the parade grounds, and we drilled every day for six months. Next, we were assigned to an old frigate, the *Furieuse*. We removed all the long cannons and replaced them with twelve 36-calibre and two 18-calibre cannons.[10] That was all the battery the frigate carried, for it was rigged *en flute;* that is, it was lightly armed so that it could carry additional cargo.

Then we were ordered to haul the frigate onto the roadstead, after which we were brought bombs, shot, and all kinds of ammunition for combat. Afterwards, two thousand barrels of flour, water, and provisions were loaded onto the frigate.

We sailed in a squadron of three ships of the line

[warships] with eighty-two cannons each, the *Cour-ageux, d'Hautpoult,* and the *Polonais;* three first-class frigates, including *L'Italienne* and the *Bellause;* and one other small frigate, the *Félicité.*

To the West Indies Again

I n the summer of 1809, during the Peninsular War, Britain was also threatening the French colonies in the West Indies, especially Martinique[1] and Guadeloupe,[2] which France intended to keep at all costs.

At this time, Bourneuf's squadron was preparing to sail to the West Indies, to deliver supplies and troops. Before leaving, however, it had to run a British blockade off the coast of France. Bourneuf briefly describes a skirmish that took place off Les Sables d'Olonne. His frigate did not take part, but the battle cost France the three "first-class" frigates in the squadron. He also recounts other clashes at sea, which end with his capture and the beginning of his adventures in Nova Scotia.

1. Martinique became a French colony in 1635, and it is now a department of France, sending three deputies to the National Assembly. The island's population is about 360,000, mainly black, and its chief mainstays are sugar cane and rum.

2. Guadeloupe, located about three hundred miles south of Puerto Rico, is a group of seven islands with a population of about 350,000. Colonized by the French about the same time as Martinique, it, too, is a French department. It was briefly occupied by the British, in 1759 and 1815. In addition to rum and sugar cane, coffee and cocoa are its chief industries.

THE THREE FRIGATES AWAITED US in the open sea, but the British fleet discovered them. The British fleet was a superior force, so the crews of the frigates did not think that it was wise to risk a battle. The wind was also against them, preventing them from entering Port Louis, where the three ships of the line were located. The frigates tried to reach Rochefort but were pursued by the British, who caught up with them and even went ahead of them.

To escape, the crews beached the frigates in a cove called Blanc Sablon. There were no forts at Blanc Sablon, so fearing that the British were going to capture them, the men set fire to their ships.

The remainder of the French fleet, the three ships of the line and the two small frigates, was still at Lorient.

Main forward deck of a French ship of the line, a square-rigged three-decker with guns on all three decks.

We set sail for our destination, and we reached Les Saintes [Iles des Saintes] without incident.

The pilots took us into port, where there was a good harbour between three islands that formed a tripod. Two of these islands were inhabited, but the other one was deserted, having only brambles, wild oranges, and other fruit. There was a fort on each island. We disembarked some of our troops, and the rest of the fleet disembarked all of their troops at Guadeloupe.

When the British received news that we were at Les Saintes, they signalled all their units in the Windward Islands and sent couriers everywhere. In three days, we were tightly blockaded. Any ship that attempted to leave port—there were three passages—would have been captured.

The British fleet comprised more than forty sails,[3] and all were full of troops. Some of the troops disembarked on the uninhabited island and built forts and blinds. The French troops that had gone ashore attacked them, and a number of skirmishes followed. As they were only a quarter of a league from us, we could see them fall, both French and English. Every day, our troops attacked, then retired to the safety of the forts on the islands. They repeated this manoeuvre daily for fifteen days.

The British warships unloaded mortars and cannons, bombs and shot and powder. After the British had built their forts, they began to bomb us. Bombs[4] were falling all around and exploding. The three French ships, though armed with eighty-two cannons each, were helpless. The British troops were on high ground, so our cannonballs could not reach them. It would have been a waste of ammunition.

When the captains of the French vessels realized this, they held a council of war. They decided that as soon as night came, the three ships of the line would sail without making a sound. The wind was favourable, and they

3. The word "sail" usually referred to a ship, but Bourneuf is exaggerating about the number of vessels. The British fleet, large by contemporary standards, consisted of twenty-three ships, including five frigates, thirteen corvettes, or other small warships, and five ships of the line. The five ships of the line were the Neptune, with 108 guns; the York, the Pompée, and the Captain, with 82 guns each; and the Polyphemus, with 74 guns. The head of the fleet was Rear Admiral Cochrane.

4. The bombs of a 36-calibre cannon were 6 inches in diameter and weighed 36 pounds; a 24-calibre cannon, 5 inches in diameter and 24 pounds; an 18-calibre cannon, 4 inches in diameter.

set sail when it was dark. The British on the island got wind of what was happening and shot rockets into the air to notify their fleet of the direction that our ships were taking. Almost the whole British fleet pursued them.

About an hour after the ships had left, we heard cannon shots and saw fire in the distance, but there was no battle. Three days later, the British caught up with *d'Hautpoult,* and a battle began. It was three against one, and more British ships arrived. The battle lasted about an hour, and finally, *d'Hautpoult* lowered its flag. The *Polonais* and the *Courageux,* which sailed faster than *d'Hautpoult,* reached France safely and anchored in the basin of Cherbourg.

The *Furieuse* and the *Félicité* left Les Saintes the day following the departure of the three warships. We went to Basse Terre, Guadeloupe, and during the twenty-mile voyage, an enemy vessel tried to cut us off. But it did not have a large enough crew to attack us. The crew fired a few volleys and cut some of our rigging but did not kill any of us. The British ship did not dare come any closer, as we were under the protection of a large fort. We soon reached Basse Terre, where there were four or five big forts.

At Basse Terre, we anchored the *Furieuse* and the *Félicité,* with one anchor in the harbour and one on land. We also tied them to a large wharf. The remaining troops on board disembarked, and after, we unloaded the ammunition and the flour. Then we removed the rigging to inspect the frigates and to do any necessary repairs. Finally, we started to reload in preparation for sailing back to France.

The British, however, did not give us time to do much of anything. They approached the harbour every two days, and there were always seventeen sails out there when the weather was good. Day and night, they arrived, ready to fire on us. They did not want us to

return to France; they were bent on destroying us.

We got little sleep at night, or we slept on deck with our guns and our bayonets ready. The cannoneers slept alongside their posts. Whenever the weather permitted, we sent two lifeboats outside the harbour to spy on the enemy and to give an alarm with gunpowder when they saw enemy ships or shallops[5] coming towards us. When the British realized that they had been discovered, they turned back. After this had happened a few times, they did not come so often.

Once, however, they brought a large brig full of cannons, its sails covered with sulphur, gunpowder, and tar and its deck and hold filled with barrels of gunpowder. The British towed it as close to us as they dared, and they tried with chains and grappling hooks to grab our ropes. The wind was pushing the brig towards us, and if it had brushed against us and exploded, we would have all perished. As soon as it approached, however, we opened fire. It blew up, pieces of it falling on our deck, and sank. Some of the fragments were large, and it was a miracle that no one was injured.

The British continued to harass us, but after the "fireboat" had blown up, they did not bother us so much. We began to load the frigates with molasses and sugar.

5. *A "shallop" is a large schooner-rigged boat with two masts, or more commonly, it is a light vessel with a small mainmast and a foremast with lug sails.*

We had received orders to prepare to leave as part of another squadron. The fleet was sent as many troops and officers as it could accommodate. Meanwhile, there were always seventeen British sails watching our every move, as a cat watches a mouse.

When the Admiral gave the signal, the three frigates in the roadstead left port to wait for us at sea. Our two small frigates and the three warships, without the British noticing, left port one dark and rainy night. On departing, the *Furieuse* ran aground on a sand bar, where she remained for a whole tide. We floated free the following day and set sail.

We soon saw enemy ships gaining on us. The *Félicité* did not sail so well as the *Furieuse,* and the British captured it. The *Félicité* had defended itself, but it had only fourteen cannons, and two frigates[6] were firing on it at the same time. So it had to lower its flag. One cannot do anything against a superior force.

Nothing of note happened to our frigate until it reached the Grand Banks of Newfoundland. There, we spotted a large vessel, and our captain and our officers held a council of war and decided to chase it, thinking it was a merchant ship with a large and valuable cargo.

We pursued the ship for thirty hours without gaining on it. Then suddenly, the hunters became the hunted: a large British frigate appeared on the horizon and began to pursue us.

The chase lasted for some thirty hours. When we saw the ship gaining on us, we hove to and prepared for battle. The captain gave us some wine mixed with powder, and we fought the British frigate for six and three-quarter hours.[7] We lost seventeen men, and sixty were wounded. I was shot in the leg; the Captain received a bullet in the stomach, and it came out by his shoulder blade; and one officer had a leg cut off.

In the course of the battle, our masts were blown away, and all our rigging was broken. The *Furieuse,* in

6. The Furieuse *and the* Félicité *left Basse Terre on the night of June 14, 1809. They were hotly pursued by the British, and on June 18, the* Felicité *was overtaken by the* Latona, *under Captain Hugh Pigot. The* Latona *was armed with twenty-eight 18-calibre cannons and two 32-calibre carronades.*

7. *On July 5, the British sloop the* Bonne Citoyenne, *under William Mounsey, began chasing the* Furieuse *in the mid-Atlantic. On July 6, the* Bonne Citoyenne,

pitiful shape, was full of cannonball holes. The frigate took in a lot of water, but as the sea was calm, the British plugged the holes.

It took twenty-seven days to reach Halifax. When we arrived, the British took the officers to nearby Preston, on their word of honour that they would not leave, and the rest of the men were incarcerated in the prison on Melville Island. The wounded were taken to the hospital at the dockyard. I remained there for forty days. My leg swelled as big as my body, and I could not walk for a long time.

	Tons	Guns	Broadside (in feet)	Men	Killed	Wounded
Bonne Citoyenne	511	20	297	127	1	5
Furieuse	1,085	20	279	200	35*	60?

* Bourneuf's figure, 17, was low.

the superior vessel, began steering a zigzag course, discharging all the cannons on each side in turn. With skilful manoeuvring, the ship managed 129 of these "broadsides" in seven hours; the Furieuse, only 70. As a result, the British vessel's carronades were protected from overheating. Its ammunition was exhausted, however, so the ship moved athwart the Furieuse's hawse, and the British prepared to board. At that time, the French crew began firing. Although both vessels were severely damaged, the Furieuse was forced to surrender.

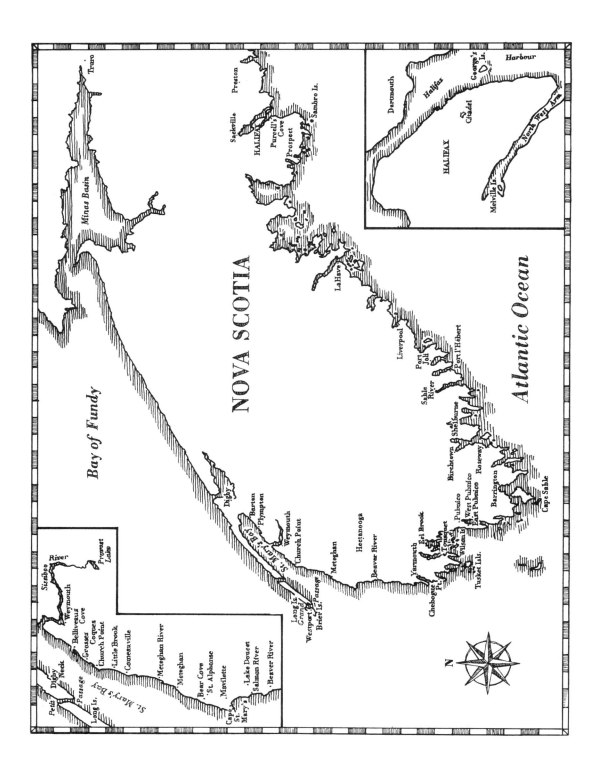

Truro

Preston

Sackville

HALIFAX

Purcell's Cove

Prospect

Sambro Is.

Minas Basin

NOVA SCOTIA

La Have

Liverpool

Port Joli

Port l'Hébert

Sable River

Birchtown

Shelburne

Roseway

West Pubnico

Pubnico

East Pubnico

Barrington

Cape Sable

Bay of Fundy

Atlantic Ocean

Digby

Barten

Plympton

Weymouth

Church Point

Meteghan

Hectanooga

Beaver River

Yarmouth

Eel Brook

Tusket

Wilson Is.

Tusket Isls.

Cheboque Pt.

Long Is.

Grand Passage

Westport

Brier Is.

St. Mary's Bay

Dartmouth

Halifax

Citadel

George's Is.

North West Arm

Melville Is.

HALIFAX

Harbour

Sissiboo River

Propsect Lake

Petit Passage

Digby Neck

Long Is.

Cape St. Mary's

Weymouth

Belliveaus Cove

Grosses Coques

Church Point

Little Brook

Comeauville

Meteghan River

Meteghan

Bear Cove

St. Alphonse

Mavilette

Lake Doucet

Salmon River

Beaver River

St. Mary's Bay

N

Imprisoned on Melville Island

During the Napoleonic Wars, French prisoners in the New World were incarcerated on Melville Island, on the south side of the North West Arm in Halifax. Although Bourneuf says that the island covers twenty acres—he is prone to exaggeration—it actually spans four.

Melville Island was first known as Kavanagh Island, after James Kavanagh, who purchased it from John Butler Kelly in April 1784. According to H. Meredith Logan, in "Melville Island, The Military Prison of Halifax," Kavanagh Island was first used as a place of interment for prisoners of war in August 1803. In 1804, Kavanagh sold the island to the British for one thousand pounds, and its name was changed to Melville, after Viscount Melville, First Lord. In 1808, the main prison was built, and during the War of 1812, it housed American prisoners, as well as French. After the downfall of Napoleon

and the Treaty of Ghent, which ended the War
of 1812, all prisoners of war were returned to
their native countries. Then, Melville Island was
used to house black slaves that had deserted their
masters and sought refuge with British troops.
The island belonged to the Royal Navy until
1856, when it became an army prison. The last
prisoner, a Private Morton of the Royal Canadian Regiment, was discharged on May 28,
1909.

The British penal system in Nova Scotia was
harsh during the early 1800s, and civilians
charged with a crime were speedily convicted
and punished. The lash was the penalty for the
least offences. In the town of Shelburne, for
example, Sylvia Gracey, a woman convicted of
petit larceny, received forty lashes, save one with
a cat-o'-nine-tails, on her bare back and was
sentenced to the house of correction. John
Windsor, a black who had run away from a
workhouse, was sent to the house of correction
and received ten lashes on arrival and every
Monday for two months. In addition, he was
sentenced to hard labour, his leg chained to a log
to prevent his running away.

Hanging was the typical punishment for mur-
der, stealing, and killing someone else's sheep.
For lesser offences, such as defamation of charac-
ter, there were pillories and whipping posts,
found in every town and in some villages.

However, from Bourneuf's account of his three years on Melville Island and his brief imprisonment in Shelburne jail, it appears that the treatment of war prisoners was far more lenient. No doubt, his experiences influenced his decision to stay in Nova Scotia and become a British subject.

1. *A "doubloon" was a Spanish gold coin that was widely used in the New World in the 1700s. Its value equalled sixteen silver dollars.*

2. *Father Jean-Mandé Sigogne was a Catholic priest exiled to England during the French Revolution. He was pastor of St. Mary's Parish at Church Point, Nova Scotia, from 1799 until his death in 1844. He was also pastor of Cape Sable and, when in that parish, resided at Eel Brook, now known as Ste. Anne du Ruisseau.*

3. *By the time Bourneuf wrote his memoirs, Nova Scotia had adopted the dollar as its currency. In 1809-10, transactions would have been made in pounds.*

4. *Bourneuf is referring to the money that the prisoners made from selling their wares.*

IN THE HOSPITAL AT THE DOCKYARD, there was a young man from Granville, France, who died of his wounds. A cannonball had entered his thigh and blown off part of his abdomen, so that you could see his intestines. He had three half-doubloons[1] and a nice watch that he gave me, asking me to have a mass said for him. I kept the promise and had Father Sigogne[2] celebrate the mass as soon as I settled in St. Mary's Bay.

After I recovered, I was taken to Melville Island, to join the other prisoners. When I arrived, all the Frenchmen were working. Some were knitting stockings, mitts, gloves, or purses, and some were spinning. Some were making model battleships rigged with silk and armed with cannons made from pennies. It took almost six months to make some of these models, and they sold for as much as twenty dollars.[3]

Other Frenchmen made hats from birchbark, all kinds of crafts from bones, such as snuff boxes, knives, forks, dice, dominoes, and even ships. The French prisoners bought more than a thousand leg bones from butchers in Halifax, paying five shillings for each group of one hundred.

Among the prisoners were painters, jewellers, shoemakers, carpenters, schoolteachers, dancing masters, and music masters. Each worked at his trade: there were no idlers, or at least very few.

The prisoners got supplies through the jailer. They gave him money[4] in advance, and he kept a sort of shop where he sold almost everything the inmates needed: bread, butter, potatoes, lime, soap, rice, pepper, thread, needles, and onions. When a prisoner asked for something he did not have, he wrote it down and picked it up when he went into town. For example, he brought more than five thousand pounds of wool a year, and he did not charge high prices.

When a prisoner went to the woods to get something he needed, such as Labrador tea or birchbark, he

Melville Island, Halifax. Lieutenant J.F. Bland, The Illustrated London News, *May 19, 1855.*

was escorted by soldiers. Some prisoners made nets,[5] and under guard, they set them in the harbour at night and raised them in the morning.

When I arrived at the prison, I had fifty dollars. I did not spend my money right away. Instead, I observed my fellow prisoners and started to work between the hours of my school.[6]

The first thing I did was unravel my white nightcap, which my sister had knit for me three years earlier. I wound the wool into a ball, and I asked one of my companions to show me how to knit, which he did with pleasure. I had a hook made so that I could knit gloves. It took me a long time to make the first pair. Even though the wool was old, I washed the gloves and dyed them and put them on forms. They looked as if they had been made with new wool, and I sold them. I no longer had a nightcap for sleeping.

I bought wool and continued this trade for three months. Then I noticed that the prisoners who made things from bones were earning far more than the others. I learned this skill and became an associate with three other young men who were very talented craftsmen and who were very practical. After I joined them, I became fluent enough in English to sell all the articles

5. *At that time, nets were made with coarse cotton thread.*

6. *Apparently, Bourneuf tutored some of his fellow prisoners, but his "school" is not mentioned elsewhere in his autobiography.*

we made. I set up two small stores, or counters, on tables. I tended one store, and for a shilling, Dominique Valmanda tended the other. He is now living in Halifax and earns his living by painting houses.

Every night, we picked up our merchandise, in boxes that were specially made. There were more than twenty tables; other workers sold many little things from a box hanging from their neck.

The British visited us in large groups. There were many warships and large numbers of troops in Halifax, and few of these officers did not come to visit us. Along with their ladies, they came during the week, and work-men, clerks, and tradesmen came on Sundays. We received contracts from ladies, from officers, from jewellers, from shoemakers, from people who made nice rings with hair, from painters, and from men who worked with ivory.

The prison was like a small town fair. We held lotter-ies, often more than twenty. We marked cards with names of articles, sold them for three sous each, then drew the cards from bags. One could win prizes such as a big warship made with bones, worth twenty dollars, a box of dominoes, a teaspoon, ivory toothpicks, or shaving brushes. Some won every time they played, and the objects on the table tempted them to play and spend more. Sometimes people got prizes worth a lot more than they had risked, and that encouraged their companions to spend more money, too.

When the weather was fine, we could take in more than one hundred pounds a day. Each prisoner's share was small, however, because there were sometimes more than five hundred prisoners.

Some prisoners had been there for twelve years, others ten. When the prison was full, the authorities put some of the inmates on transports bound for England.

During the French Revolution, up to the time of the Little Peace in 1802 [Treaty of Amiens], prisons in

Halifax filled up many times. The British government kept prisoners at Halifax for the gainful employment of officials as, for example, surgeons, jailers, butchers, bakers, and others. That is why some had been there for a long time. They liked it because they were well paid and well fed. A few inmates took a great deal of money back to France.

Generally, the French are more frugal than the British or the Americans. I know that by experience. When I was at the prison, the gentlemen and the ladies who came did not value twenty dollars more than we value one dollar at present.[7] In France, a poor man could not save any money because wages were too low. Carpenters who worked in the Empire's shipyards, for example, received only twenty French sous, the equivalent of ten pence, and they had to pay for their own board, and they had to be good workers at that. All other tradesmen were paid on the same scale. Farm labourers made only twenty *écus*[8] per year.

The best sailors made only six gourds,[9] and the worst only three. When I was on the warship, a sailor was paid every six months, but not until he had all the clothes prescribed by law.[10] Nearly every sailor sent money home to his parents. There were a few who spent all that they had. A French sailor, whether on warships or on merchant ships, is usually a drunkard. Nonetheless, he is highly esteemed in battle, for it is believed that a drunkard is usually a better fighter than a sober man. A drunkard fears nothing: he throws caution to the wind.

As for French women, the best workers earned only ten *écus* a year. Seamstresses who went from house to house earned only five sous, the equivalent of two and a half pence. This is why I think the French are so frugal. When they do lay their hands on money, they do not like to part with it.

Melville Prison is on a little island that covers twenty

7. *During the Napoleonic Wars, the economy of Halifax was booming, not the case when Bourneuf was writing his memoirs.*

8. *An écu equalled half a crown, and a crown was worth five silver dollars.*

9. *A "gourd" was a silver dollar.*

10. *This law was intended to prevent a sailor from selling part of his uniform; it forced him to be responsible for it.*

Melville Island from the N.E. *J.E. Woolford,* Sketches in Nova Scotia, 1817.

acres [four acres]. A bridge on the south side connects the island to the mainland, and a boat on the east side brings all of the provisions, the soldiers, and many of the visitors.

The prison itself was on the west side of the island. It was about three hundred feet long, eighty feet wide, and thirty feet high. The hospital, the jailer's quarters, and the interpreter's lodging were upstairs. The interpreter was a Frenchman, and he worked closely with the doctor, receiving a monthly salary. He also interpreted all other communications with the prisoners.

The prison was divided lengthwise into three parts. In the centre was a common area for prisoners, for walking, for setting up their shops and counters, and for the dancing masters to exercise. At night, there was a place to put large tubs that contained our necessities. Men hired by the government removed these tubs, and, I believe, they received two gourds per month. They took the garbage to the harbour through a large door intended for this purpose. There was also a place to wash our feet and to wash fish. We had all the fish we needed, for we could fish ourselves or buy from English fishermen who came to the prison to sell their catch.

The other parts were divided every eight feet into "ports," each of which housed thirty inmates. In each port, there were posts that reached the ceiling, and between the posts were cross-pieces, about six feet apart, to which we attached our hammocks. There also were smaller cross-pieces that served as ladders to our hammocks. Those who slept higher up risked breaking their necks, but they got used to it. Every night, we hung our hammocks, and every morning, we took them down, carrying them outside when the weather was fine. We carried in our own water, from the other side of the bridge, with armed guards escorting us there and back.

The prison yard was enclosed by pointed stakes that were twelve to fifteen feet high and that were supported by cross-pieces. We fished through the space between the posts. We caught moles, which were abundant at high tide. They were after the garbage that came from the yard or from elsewhere and flowed out from around the posts, which were three-quarters awash at high tide. Along the posts in the lowest areas were four outhouses that the sea cleaned at high tide.

On the other side were the guards' barracks, the magazines, and the officers' lovely house.

The hospital yard was on the western side. The hospital provided bedspace for one hundred, but I never saw it full. Nor was there ever a serious illness among the men. Many prisoners went to the hospital to get a quart of wine, allotted each day for ten sous, or five pence. Dr. Hude,[11] of Halifax, knew full well that the men were not sick, but he seldom refused, unless they had too much to drink and were a nuisance.

The prison was a healthy place. There were very few deaths; inmates were buried in the cemetery on the other side of the bridge.

The kitchen opened onto the northeastern end of the hospital yard. There was a large pot to heat water to wash our clothes, and there was hot water every fore-noon for those who wanted to wash. We received wood and coal for the kitchen, and in winter, we received two large stoves and coal to keep us warm in the prison.

11. *There is no record of a Dr. Hude in Halifax at that time. Bourneuf's writing, however, is hard to decipher in this instance.*

Our soup was cooked in two large pots. In addition, we each received half a pound of meat per day, which was weighed by the butcher. The inmates were divided into groups of seven, and each group had an eighteen-inch-long spit with a number. The meat was tied on the spit with string. When it was done, the cook, paid eight dollars a month, took a long iron fork and put it into wooden tubs. Then he rang a bell, and each prisoner approached with his wooden bowl. Using a large copper ladle, the cook gave each inmate a spoonful of broth and his ration of meat.

We received our supplies of meat, bread, potatoes, and salt every second day. The butcher, who had the government contract, brought the meat, and the baker, also under contract to the government, brought the bread. The baker had a store outside the prison, near the barracks.

To cut the meat, we formed a committee of two prisoners, not always the same two. If the meat or the bread was not good, we made the butcher or the baker bring supplies of better quality. This happened many times. A few times, the meat looked like drowned dog, and the bread could have stuck to a wall. It was not the government's fault, however: it was the contractor's.

After we complained, we were brought good victuals, but we often remained two days without food. If we had not taken action, the contractors would have brought worse and worse food. We had an advantage over them, for if we refused the supplies, commissioners[12] were appointed to investigate. Contractors tendered to provide supplies.

The jailer, and the soldiers on guard duty, counted the prisoners every morning and every evening, on going out and coming in. If they made a mistake, they counted us a second time. Sometimes a prisoner escaped during a blizzard, over the ice in the harbour. Many we never saw again or never knew what happened to them.

12. *The British appointed commissioners to oversee the operations of the prison.*

When someone escaped, we were kept in all day, and if the soldiers found out who had helped him, they punished them.

Some inmates went to a nearby mill[13] to drink rum, and they were always accompanied by soldiers. Many prisoners waited for their chance, then got the soldiers drunk, and escaped. Often, however, they were recaptured.

Soldiers who allowed a prisoner to escape were severely punished. And after an escape, the officers refused all prisoner requests to leave the prison, but within a few days, they usually relented and began granting permission again.

Men who were recaptured were put in a hole in the cellar under the prison. The hole had iron bars, and one could see daylight through a small opening above the door. Men in the hole were fed only bread and water. The other prisoners, however, feeling generous towards their compatriots, deprived themselves of portions of their meat and soup rations and shared them with those who had deserted.

Some prisoners were recaptured after spending fifteen days in the woods, eating only wild berries. They often came back with their clothes torn. Right away a raffle was held among the other inmates to provide them with new clothes.

Even though the other prisoners were restricted because of those who had tried to escape, they never reproached them. On the contrary, they regarded them with high esteem, for a Frenchman who demonstrated courage by attempting to gain freedom was admired more than one who did not try at all.

There were always five or six sentinels on duty. If they heard a noise inside the prison, they fired a shot to sound the alarm. Then the Captain would come with a detachment of soldiers to see what was the matter. If prisoners were fighting, they were put in the hole.

13. *To the north, there was a mill owned by a family named Hosterman. Perhaps this was the mill the prisoners visited.*

In 1811, two years after I was confined to Melville Prison, the jailer asked for twenty men to go and work on the road to Truro. I was twenty-four years old and was becoming quite bored in jail. I obtained permission to go. A schooner from the dockyard took us to Sackville. That night, we slept aboard the ship, and I almost died from flea bites. The next day, we arrived at our destination, twenty-seven miles from Halifax [by boat], and we were assigned to cabins, ten men to each. At night, we walked about two miles up the road to see what it looked like: we had not come here to work but to escape. After we returned from our walk, we received enough food for eight days.

Escape, Capture, and Escape

As Bourneuf has pointed out, prisoners volunteered to work on road crews for two reasons: to alleviate the boredom of incarceration and to seize an opportunity to escape (escaping from Melville Prison was nearly impossible). Using prisoners on work crews not only benefited the inmates but also the government and the public, which bore much of the responsibility for road building.

The first roads in Nova Scotia were built largely by the settlers themselves. For example, Bonaventure Deveau and his brother Olivier had to clear their own road to Bonaventure's property at Hectanooga, in the Township of Clare and five miles from the nearest settlement. After 1783, public roads came under the jurisdiction of the General Sessions of the Peace for the county. People petitioned this court for a road, and after deliberation, the court rejected or accepted the petition. The Legislative Assembly granted sums of money for the improvement of roads and often required "freeholders," or land owners, to carry out "statute labour," that is, to work a certain number of days, without pay, in the construction or maintenance of roads or on other public projects. Failure to fulfil an order often resulted in a fine. Consequently, the land owners, taken away from their farms or other sources of livelihood, welcomed the assistance of prisoners of war. As Bourneuf shows, the inhabitants of Prospect and Purcell's Cove warmly received him and his fellow prisoners. Bourneuf went to work on the Prospect Road in 1812, his second stint on a road crew.

During his first experience, Bourneuf tried unsuccessfully to escape while his road crew was working at Truro.

THERE WERE FORTY SOLDIERS to work with us during
the day and to guard us during the night. One night, it
rained heavily until about ten o'clock. When the rain
subsided, two fellow prisoners and I took our ration of
bread and left the camp without the soldiers noticing.
One of my companions was older than I; the other,
younger.

We walked all night. My shoes hurt my feet, so I
took them off and walked barefoot; the road, being
newly cleared, was very rough. The next day, at sunrise,
we hid near the main highway to see whether the soldiers were pursuing us. However, the soldiers went by
without our seeing them and hid under a bridge to wait
for us.

When night fell, we walked out of the woods and
continued on our way. We had planned to go to
Chaleur Bay, but at midnight, we arrived at the bridge
where the soldiers were hiding. They jumped on us like
dogs on their prey, and they took us to a large inn near
the bridge. There, my companions lay down on the
floor and slept for about an hour.

I was so tired that I lay down outside. The soldiers,
five of them, got me up and prepared to leave. I told
them that I was sick and that I could not walk. They did
not believe me and kicked me, and prodded me with
their bayonets so much that I thought they were going

to kill me. Even though I was sick, I was forced to leave. We walked about thirty-eight miles that day. Along the way, the soldiers told us that they had followed us the night before and that they had known approximately where we had entered the woods.

Finally, we arrived back at the work site. After breakfast the next day, we headed for Halifax in the company of a sergeant and four soldiers. We did not enter the town. Instead, we took the road that led directly to Melville Island.

When we left Truro, the Sergeant and the four soldiers had no money and no provisions. We shared our eight days' supply of food with them, and they asked to borrow money. As they had handled me roughly when I was ill, I gave them twenty shillings, not expecting to see it again. But after a few days, the Sergeant gave me back the money.

As soon as we arrived at Melville Prison, my two companions and I were placed in the hole and were confined there for ten days, eating only bread and water. Our comrades were pleased to see us again but were sad that we had been captured. As Frenchmen are generous and sympathetic in these circumstances, they shared their rations of meat and soup with us.

When prisoners intended to escape, they began their preparations in advance. They told only their best friends and swore them to the utmost secrecy. If the secret was divulged, the culprit was stoned, not by just one person. He was taken to a place well hidden from the English and bound, and the whole company carried out the sentence that the Grand Council[1] of the prisoners had decided—stoned until dead.

Often, quarrels erupted among the prisoners, and fights broke out. When the British overheard the commotion, they came with guards, who took the fighters and placed them in the hole for a while.

Once, two Frenchmen tried to escape. They hid

1. The "Grand Council" was made up of respected prisoners who maintained a sort of discipline over their compatriots.

under one of the outhouses in the prison yard and waited for nightfall to make their getaway over the ice. When the soldiers counted us that night, they noticed that two men were missing.

The jailer and the officers searched for them in every nook and cranny. They finally found them in their uncomfortable and miserable hiding place. The unfortunate would-be escapees were in a pitiful state. They were put in the hole in their stinking clothes, and they remained in them all night.

The next morning, fellow prisoners gave them a change of clothing and took them a large tub of water and some soap so that they could wash. After that, they smelled better.

Following our ten days in the hole, we resumed our work at the prison, with our supplies, our tables, and even our lotteries. I continued these commercial ventures for a year, along with my three associates, whom I spoke of earlier. There was a fifth member of our group, an old man who did our cooking, and for his pay, he ate with us. The government cook prepared only one meal a day, so the prisoners cooked stews over small fires in the lee of the wind, in the most convenient places in the prison yard. There were a few youths who were not very saving or wise: they ate two days' rations at one meal and remained whole days without food.

Men made money much as they had before: there were very few who were lazy. Some prisoners did laundry for other inmates, who paid them. A few inmates brewed spruce beer, which they sold for a sou a glass. Others caught fish, cod and mackerel, which they sold for a sou apiece; made butter, which they formed into small balls that sold for a sou apiece; bought potatoes by the bushel, cooked them, and sold them for a sou or two apiece; or made candy from sugar and molasses that they sold for a sou apiece. Still others had game tables for card playing, dice, and billiards of sorts. Some inmates sold their clothes, even their bedding and their hammocks, to gamble.

We continued to make hats of birchbark. We sold thousands of them to merchants, who sent them to the colonies for black slaves.[2] As well, we knitted woolen gloves for all the troops. Sergeants contracted for as many as ten thousand pairs a year.

Among us were many tradesmen. Tailors and shoemakers made goods for Halifax gentlemen; a number of prisoners went out to work as domestics for households in Halifax; and masons plied their trade, making stone walls around the gardens of houses between the prison and the city.

Many prisoners kept animals. Some had hens that fed on scraps, and they sold their eggs to the city for two shillings, six pence, a dozen. The hens were housed in cabins, made of stone and earth, that were located in the prison yard. Some men had pigs, which also fed on scraps. One man had raised a kitten that danced like a monkey and meowed at its master's command. This cat always slept with its master.

Although the prisoners were enterprising, some did not earn as much as three sous per day. But somehow they managed to buy their necessities, such as tobacco, thread, needles, soap, and other items to keep themselves clean. They did not have to worry about their clothes. The British government gave clothing to those who needed it, and I believe that the French government reimbursed the British for this.[3] Our footwear was a type of galoshes, with wooden soles, upper parts made of all kinds of old clothes and bedding and, sometimes, tops made of ropes sewn together.

In 1812, I received permission to go and work on the Prospect Road. Twenty or thirty of us were divided into teams of ten or twelve, and we worked under British overseers. Our food was brought from Melville Prison twice a week, and we slept in the overseers' houses.

2. *At this time, slavery was still universal in the British and French colonies, including Nova Scotia. In* King's Bounty, *Marion Robertson gives numerous examples of Loyalists in Shelburne owning slaves.*

3. *Bourneuf presumes that the French government reimbursed the British, but there is no evidence of this.*

I remained there for three months, earning one shilling, three pence, a day. On Sundays, we visited each other. One week, we visited our companions in their lodgings, and the next week, they visited us. Some Sundays, we went to see our fellow inmates at the prison; other weeks, we went to Mass at Prospect.

We also went fishing. Fishermen lent us their boats, their lines, and their bait and even told us where to drop our lines. We went to those areas, but nary a cod did we take. My adventurous companions with whom I had tried to escape the previous year were still with me. We were not out to catch fish but to get the lay of the harbour to plan our next escape.

But we continued to work on the public highway for some time. Then, one time, we ordered more bread than usual. The provisions arrived on Saturday, and on Sunday, we went to see our comrades, who were working about a league away. We spent the day with them, and that evening, we told them that we were going to leave by sea. We bade them *adieu*.

Having returned to our lodgings, we remained until nightfall and then took the Prospect Road. There was an island named Purcell's Island,[4] and on it was a house and many fishermen who had small boats. I had already noticed that fact.

When we arrived at the seashore, I took off some of

4. *Purcell's Island is a small island in Purcell's Cove. No doubt, it was named after the Purcell whose boat Bourneuf and his companions stole.*

my clothes and swam to the boats on the island. I took one, as well as the sails of another so that we had a spare set. I returned to the shore to get my clothes and my companions. I held the boat still with an oar while my friends put the clothes in bags. I asked them if they had everything, and they answered yes. We then shoved off, and we rowed, all three of us, until we were a good distance from land.

When I started to put my clothes back on, I noticed that my companions had left them ashore. I therefore lost not only a bag full of good clothes but also my pocketbook, which contained precious papers and a note from Etienne Caron, a French officer who had escaped from Preston, where, on his word of honour, he was to have remained.

After leaving Purcell's Island, we followed the coast along the village of Prospect and then struck out for deep water until we lost sight of land. We were looking for American privateers,[5] for we intended to go to America. When we were forty or fifty miles from the lighthouse on Sambro Island, we set our course westward. We went that far out, because we knew that the British would be looking for us the following day.

In fact, Mr. Purcell, from whom we had stolen the boat, went to complain to the Governor the day after our departure. The Governor sent ships after us, I believe, but we did not see any of them, and none saw us. Nobody suspected that we were that far out.

We sighted land at LaHave, and at daybreak, we arrived off Liverpool. There, we found ourselves in the middle of a convoy of some thirty sailboats. They were becalmed, and we stayed among them for three or four hours. Then a slight breeze came, and we promptly sailed away. They sailed towards the east, and we continued on our westward journey. The wind was southwest, so we had to tack until we were off Shelburne.

Then a high wind rose, and fog closed in. We had to

5. A "privateer" was an armed merchant ship whose captain was supplied by his government with "letters of marque," which authorized him and his crew to attack and capture enemy ships. (Captured crews of ships with letters of marque were considered prisoners of war, not pirates.) During the War of 1812, between Britain and the United States, American privateers preyed on British merchant vessels off Nova Scotia, as well as on coastal villages from Pubnico to Isle Madame. Many Nova Scotian merchants had their ships armed and supplied with letters of marque. They, in turn, preyed on enemy ships, often with profitable results.

ride it out for two days, after which the wind died down some. But we had a headwind, and we had to tack again, until our sails ripped. Luckily, we had the spare set, which we put to good use. We continued to look for American privateers. We had been told that they were as thick as flies, but we never saw one.

After having been tossed about in our small boat for eight days, we were bruised and dirty and wet and covered with boils. Moreover, we had no fresh water, and what was left of our bread was soaked with salt water. We concluded that it was no longer feasible to try to reach the coast of America.

We noticed a schooner on the fishing banks off Shelburne. It appeared to be fifty tons, and we decided to board it. We had an old axe, a few old belaying pins, and some pieces of wood that fishermen used to kill cod.

About ten miles from the ship, having prepared our plan of attack, we each ate a piece of bread, for we were hungry. With a tailwind, we set sail. As we approached the ship, we saw that the crew was pulling in cod hand over hand.

When we got closer, the fishermen noticed that we intended to board. They left their lines and prepared to defend themselves. They had a gun and a sword, and they forbade us to come any closer. They told us to take off for the open sea, but we explained that we wanted fish and water. Then they let us approach. However, they kept their gun, their sword, and their belaying pins ready while we were alongside. They gave us water and half a halibut. We asked them where we could find a good harbour, and they suggested Port Hébert.[6] We did not try to board after all—there were eight big Scotsmen—so we pushed on towards land and wished them good luck.

6. *Some maps of Nova Scotia also use the name Port Hébert, but the most common spelling is "Port l'Hébert." In the same area of the South Shore, on two headlands between Port Joli and Sable River, there is also East Port l'Hébert and Lower Port l'Hébert.*

Recaptured

In his memoirs, Bourneuf discusses two visits to Shelburne, one as a recaptured prisoner in 1812 and the other as a mate aboard the Catherine in 1816. His fortunes had improved by then, but those of the town had not.

Governor John Parr named the town Shelburne in 1783, after the Second Earl of Shelburne, Prime Minister of Britain at the end of the American Revolution. The town was to be home to about ten thousand United Empire Loyalists, but as Marion Robertson notes in her book King's Bounty, some bitterly resented the name, for they felt that the Prime Minister had not done enough to protect their interests during peace negotiations after the war.

The founders of Shelburne had great expectations for the town. An elaborate plan was drafted, with eleven long streets parallel to the harbour and sixteen shorter streets at right angles to the waterfront. Although the population of Shelburne surpassed that of Halifax for a short while, it was rapidly declining by the late 1780s.

Town of Shelburne.
J.E. Woolford,
Sketches in Nova
Scotia, 1817.

Shelburne lacked most of the pre-requisites for a successful settlement. The area was not suited to agriculture, as the soil was too shallow and too rocky. Nor was it suited to the schooner fishery. Even though the harbour was deep and almost ice free, it was too long and too far away from good fishing grounds. The founders had hoped that Shelburne would also become a naval base, but the harbour mouth was too wide to defend.

Many Loyalists, therefore, returned to the United States or moved to other areas of Nova Scotia, as well as New Brunswick or Prince Edward Island. By 1787, there were 360 deserted homes in Shelburne, and two years later, two thirds of the town was deserted. By 1818, the population had dwindled to 300; today, it is about 2,000.

In 1812, Bourneuf would have seen a town in decay, but with some vestige of its former greatness: well-laid-out streets lined with one- and two-storey buildings with gables or with gambrel roofs, and the tall lighthouse in operation on Cape Roseway. He would have also seen, however, the deserted wooden barracks opposite the town and the nearly idle waterfront. Of course, he would have noticed every detail of the jail, where he and his companions were confined.

BY THE TIME WE REACHED LAND, it was dark. We found a little island west of Port Hébert [Port l'Hébert] where we stayed for the night. The next morning, we went ashore to buy food. We went to the first house near the shore, and it belonged to a lieutenant in the Militia. He suspected that we were Americans,[1] so he told us to enter, and he sent for the Militia forthwith.

It was breakfast time, and the whole family was at home. In the twinkling of an eye, the Militia arrived and arrested us. The men took the boat that we had stolen from old man Purcell. The mail was sent to Halifax only every two weeks, so by the time Purcell learned that his boat had been discovered and by the time he got it back, he had lost most of a summer's fishing.

After we had eaten breakfast, we were taken to Shelburne, where the county prison[2] was located. The first day, we made it to Sable River, which is near Ragged Islands. We slept there, and the following day, three militia men escorted us to Shelburne. One of the men was Sergeant Peter Spearwater,[3] who was later a member of the Legislative Assembly at the same time I was.

1. *The War of 1812 was fought mostly on the Niagara Peninsula and along the Upper Canada-United States boundary. The Maritimes had been involved mainly in the capture of five towns in Maine: Eastport, Machias, Hampden, Bangor, and Castine. At the end of the war, with the Treaty of Ghent in 1814, both sides gave back the other's territories.*

2. *At this time, there was usually one prison per county, in the shire town or county seat. The county penal system included the jail, the house of correction, the workhouse, the whipping post, and the pillory. After the municipal system of government was introduced in 1879, each town had its own jail.*

3. *Peter Spearwater was an MLA for Shelburne County from 1836 to 1847. Born in Liverpool, Nova Scotia, in 1790, he married Eliza Richardson; he died in Mahone Bay in 1855.*

To get to Shelburne, we had to cross Sable River in a small boat. The three militia men gave us their guns to hold while they manned the oars. Afterwards, I told Sergeant Spearwater never to do that again. Subsequently, they were very cold towards us.

We reached Shelburne that evening, and my two companions and I were put in jail, where we slept on camp cots without any blankets. In a few days, some Scottish ladies brought us food and blankets. They had sons in French prisons, and they had learned that we were French.

Sometimes the jail was filled with visitors: the whole time we were there, men and women of the town came to see us. Eventually, we were allowed to go wherever we wanted to, to mow, to harvest, to milk cows, to cut wood, to do any work that people requested. Every day, I milked the jailer's cow. His little girl came with me, and she caught the cow and held its horns while I did the milking.

While at Shelburne, I had a strange adventure. One day, a gentleman from Liverpool lost his suitcase. As there were no newspapers in Shelburne at that time, he advertised on posters, promising a good reward to anyone who came forth with information.

Eventually, someone noticed that a Negro[4] had articles belonging to the gentleman. The deputy sheriff was obliged to bring the Negro to jail, but he was too afraid to tackle him. So he asked me to go with him to help apprehend him. We found the Negro, and I collared him and brought him to Shelburne and put him in jail.

Soon, three Scottish gentlemen, having become friendly with my companions and me, asked us whether we wanted to go and stay with them. If we accepted, they promised to send to the Governor a request for our freedom. But as I said earlier, the mail came and went only every two weeks, and by the time we had to

4. Birchtown, near
Shelburne, has a large
black population whose
ancestors came as slaves
with the Loyalist settlers
in 1783-1784 or as
"free blacks." The free
blacks had been slaves
of "rebel" owners, and
they had joined the
British cause during
the American
Revolution in exchange
for their freedom.

leave Shelburne, the answer from the Governor had not arrived.

After six weeks in Shelburne, the Colonel of the Militia received orders to take us back to Halifax at the first opportunity. An armed corvette[5] called a "revenue cutter" was anchored in Shelburne Harbour, and a detachment of the Militia took us to the wharf, where a small sailboat took us to the corvette. It was about five hundred paces from the prison to the wharf, and no fewer than a hundred people lined the route to see us off. Some were crying, and all seemed sad to see us leave.

The following day, the ship was brought to the wharf, to take on water, and a sentinel was posted on the wharf to prevent our escape. During the day, I sent for two bottles of rum. It was late when the crew finished taking on water, then supper was prepared. I went below and took one good swig of rum and went back on deck. Then I took a new kerchief that I had in

5. A corvette was smaller
than a frigate, having
only one tier of guns on
a flush deck, and no
quarter-deck. Also, it
was ship-rigged.

my bag and lowered the two bottles to my companions, to give the whole crew a good drink. The crew saw the bottles being lowered and went below. Only the cook and the coxswain remained on deck, and eventually the coxswain went below with the rest of the crew.

At that moment, I took the opportunity to escape. I jumped into a small boat lying next to the corvette and rowed to the wharf. I tied up the boat and walked through the town. As soon as I was out of the town, I ran as fast as I could to the woods, for I knew that my absence would be noticed quickly and that a search would begin right away. I followed the road from Shelburne to Cape Negro,[6] but I had no idea where I was going. I later learned that as soon as I had left the ship, the crew started running after me in all directions.

6. *Cape Negro got its name from its shape: at sea, it resembled the head of a black man.*

A Successful Escape

As Bourneuf says, he had no idea where he was going, and it is doubtful that he knew anything about the Acadians, either. The history of Acadia was not commonly known in France at this time, except on Belle-Ile-en-Mer, a little island off the coast of Brittany and in the region of Nantes. Some Acadians had settled in those areas after 1763; most of the Acadians in Nantes went to Louisiana in 1785.

Some Acadians had returned to Nova Scotia in small groups between 1764 and 1768, mostly from the New England States. Those who settled in the Argyle district of Yarmouth County received land grants in 1767 on both sides of Pubnico Harbour, on the points of land and the islands around Tusket Bay, and in the Eel Brook area. The settlers engaged mostly in fishing, farming, and lumbering on a subsistence scale. The fishing grounds around the Tusket Islands were rich, but a few men ventured much farther out and fished off the coast of Labrador, as Bourneuf eventually discovered.

Before the Deportation, which began in 1755, the Pubnico area was known as the Cape Sable region. Father Jean-Mandé Sigogne, who had left France during the Revolution, referred to his parish in Yarmouth County as Cape Sable. When he arrived in 1799, there was one chapel at Rivière des Anguilles. When Bourneuf arrived in the Cape Sable region, Rivière des Anguilles had become Eel Brook, which is now known as Ste. Anne du Ruisseau. Pubnico was the name of the villages on Pubnico Harbour, and Tousquet, not to be confused with Tusket, was the name of the settlement now known as Wedgeport.

ABOUT TEN MILES FROM SHELBURNE, it grew so dark in the thick woods that I got lost. I soon found the road again, however, and continued on my way. I found a large flat stone and lay down on it to rest. I slept an hour or two, and when I awoke, it was lighter, and I pressed on.

At sun-up, I arrived at Cape Negro. I went to a house to buy bread, but I was scared away by two big dogs that seemed ready to eat me. So I returned to the main road. By the time I reached Barrington, at ten o'clock in the morning, I was starving, as I had left Shelburne with only two biscuits in my pockets.

I went to the first house that I saw and asked for lunch. I was told to sit down, and I was given something to eat. When I finished eating, I offered to pay for the meal, but my hosts would not take anything. The master of the household, a Mr. Harding,[1] asked me where I came from. I told him that I came from Shelburne. When he asked me where I was going, I told him that I was a poor French prisoner of war who sought to make an honest living without hurting anyone.

Mr. Harding advised me not to tell anyone who I was and that I should go to the French people who lived along the shores.

"I will tell you how to get there," he said. "But be careful, for in the nearby town, there is a gentleman[2] who is our colonel in the Militia. You will recognize him easily, as he is a large man who wears glasses. When you have passed through this town, you will find two roads. Take the one to the right."

I had not gone a hundred steps from Mr. Harding's before I met this colonel, who asked me who I was, where I was going, and where I had come from. He then asked me whether I had seen, or heard of, any American privateers, and I said no. He asked me yet another question, but I did not answer. When I found

1. *Two Harding brothers were prominent citizens of Barrington at this time.*

2. *The man was John Sargeant, Lieutenant Colonel of the Barrington Militia during the Napoleonic Wars.*

the road to the right, I ran as fast as I could to escape from the old colonel.

About three miles away, I found a small house where a widow, a Mrs. Brown, lived with her two boys, who were not home at the time. Mrs. Brown sold rum, as advertised on a sign in front of her house. I went in and asked for a glass of rum. It then started to rain. I asked for a meal, and she gave me beans, called *haricots* in France, and they were as black as soot. She charged me fifteen cents for the meal.

At two o'clock in the afternoon, the rain abated, and I left. I took a new, narrow road through the woods, and it was very muddy. About four o'clock, I arrived at Pubnico, where I took a road along the river that led to the French-speaking village of East Pubnico.

The first house I came to belonged to Simon d'Entremont,[3] but it was boarded up. The next house house was Captain John Larkin's.[4] I knocked on the door, and Mrs. Larkin, alone, asked me to come in. She told me that her husband was fishing off Labrador, and I asked her whether she would be kind enough to let me stay the night. She said yes right away.

Then I went to a nearby brook to wash up. While I was there, the maid, coming from a prayer meeting, arrived at the house and asked Mrs. Larkin "who the devil" I was. She replied that I was a French prisoner of war from Halifax. When I returned to the house, Mrs. Larkin asked me what part of France I was from, and I told her near Granville, in Normandy. "Ah, yes," she said. "There are people from your area in Tousquet, and you must go see them." She said that Tousquet was thirty miles away.

While I was at the brook, Mrs. Larkin had changed her mind about allowing me to spend the night at her home. "My dear sir," she said, "I promised I would put you up for the night, but our maid is afraid of you, and if you sleep here, she will not stay here. The day before

3. *Simon d'Entremont was the son of Benoni d'Entremont. He was elected to the Nova Scotia Legislative Assembly in 1836 and served until 1840. He married Elizabeth Larkin, and after her death, he married Elizabeth Thériault, of Belliveau Cove.*

4. *Captain John Larkin was one of the original settlers of Pubnico after 1767. He married Marie Belliveau, born in 1736, the daughter of Charles Belliveau and Marguerite Bastarache. Marie Belliveau died in 1831.*

5. *François Clermont, son of Paul Clermont, was living with his family on Wilson's Island when he was killed by the crew of an American privateer.*

yesterday, a man[5] was killed at Tousquet by the Americans, and that scared us."

She pointed to her uncle's home close by and told me to go there. Her uncle's name was Ange Amirault,[6] but no one answered the door. I then knocked at the door of Joseph Belliveau.[7] He was not home, but his wife willingly agreed to give me food and lodging.

The next day, I went back to Ange Amirault's. I met his son Marc, who asked me whether I knew how to mow. I said that I could, and he told me that he was going to cut salt hay[8] on the other side of the harbour,

at a place called Ile de Grave,[9] about three or four miles away. I accepted his invitation to go with him.

At Ile de Grave, there was a large meadow of some three hundred acres that was divided among many owners.[10] Nearly all of these gentlemen were mowing their lots when Marc and I arrived. We mowed all morning and then ate lunch.

After dinner, people asked me many questions. One man asked me whether I knew a certain lady in St. Servan.[11] I said that I had even been to her home. Then I was told that her husband, Pierre Beaumont, a Frenchman at Pubnico, was about to marry a girl from the village. I discovered that it was this girl's brother who was asking all the questions, and naturally, he was against this man's seeing his sister.

6. *Ange Amirault was the son of Jacques Amirault, who settled in the Cape Sable area before the Deportation. Ange and his wife, Nathalie Belliveau, returned to this area in 1767 and were granted land in 1771.*

7. *Joseph Belliveau was Nathalie's brother. He married Marie Osithé Bourque.*

8. *Salt hay grows on the salt marshes or tidal flats of southwestern Nova Scotia. To early settlers, it was readily available, valuable fodder for their cattle.*

9. *Situated in Pubnico Harbour, this island is still called Ile de Grave by the local inhabitants. Officially, its name is Gravel Island.*

10. *In the late 1700s in the Township of Argyle and along St. Mary's Bay, all those who acquired land grants also received small plots of salt marsh.*

11. *St. Servan, on the English Channel, was a French port of debarkation for Acadians who had been exiled to England during the Deportation.*

We mowed until the middle of the afternoon, and while we were mowing, someone else asked me whether I could teach school. I replied that I could teach French, English, arithmetic, navigation, and so forth. That very evening, a village meeting was called. I began teaching school the next day.

Life at Pubnico

Although no Acadians were rich, "the poorest lived in abundance," as Longfellow wrote in Evangeline. They salted the cod and the pollock they caught in the rich fishing grounds of Cape Sable, then shipped the fish to New England in exchange for goods they could not produce, such as iron utensils, glassware, cotton, and salt.

Most of the Acadians expelled from the Cape Sable region between 1756 and 1759 wanted their former lands back when they returned to the area in the mid-1760s. Unfortunately, however, their ancestral lands had been taken over by New England settlers. The government of Nova Scotia, therefore, granted to the heads of eighteen families five thousand acres on both sides of Pubnico Harbour. The surnames included d'Entremont, Muise, Duon, Amirault, and Belliveau, as well as a few Irish names, such as Larkin and Goodwin. Most of the d'Entremonts and the Duons settled on the west side of the harbour, while most of the Amiraults and the Belliveaus chose the east side.[1] The English-speaking families settled at the end of the harbour, now Pubnico Head.

1. In 1989, the Amiraults, d'Entremonts, D'Eons (formerly Duons), and Belliveaus accounted for 634 of 1,011 listings in the Pubnico telephone directory.

The Acadian families lived in modest frame houses and had rough barns. The houses were quite far apart and hugged the narrow road on both sides as far as the eye could see. The white sails of the small fishing schooners dotted the fine harbour, which reached six miles inland. Father Manning visited Pubnico in the early 1800s. He left the following description, quoted in A Sequel to Campbell's History of Yarmouth County, *by George S. Brown:*

> Perhaps more than any other village, Pubnico prides itself on its neat dwellings and carefully kept surroundings. It has the advantage of resident artisans in the painting and furnishing line. It insures its own vessels, does its own outfitting, and with the disappearance of all inclination to division, its future will become very bright.

Bourneuf recounts his stay in Pubnico and his visits to Eel Brook (Ste. Anne du Ruisseau) and Tousquet (Wedgeport). Although he had the highest regard for the people of Pubnico, he does not dwell on the village or its industries.

I TAUGHT SCHOOL in the house where I boarded,[2] and the children loved me like their own father. I felt as if I were in paradise, after having spent three years on warships and three years as a prisoner of war. Everybody made me feel at home, young and old, women and girls. I couldn't have been happier, not even with my own family and friends in France. Sometimes I visited other Acadian villages, and I was welcomed wherever I went.

In the winter of 1812-1813, I went with two young men, Jean and Joseph Belliveau,[3] to visit three of my compatriots who were living in Tousquet. We left on a Saturday morning, and that day, we made it as far as Eel Brook, to Pierre Bourque's.[4] That night, we visited Pierre Surette.[5]

There were many people, some fine fiddling, and plenty of liquor at Surette's. In the course of the evening, I met Pierre Beaumont, the man who had a wife in St. Servan. He was angry with me, for he had been informed that I had said that his wife was still living. I told him that I had said no such thing, that I had said only that I knew a woman by the name of Beaumont, that I had been to her house, and that she kept an inn. Beaumont was the fiddler that night, and he came right up to me. He was half drunk, and you could not reason with him. He wanted to fight right then and there, but other guests stopped him. Some time after this encounter, Beaumont's wife tried to join him in St. Pierre and Miquelon, but she perished in a shipwreck, along with all of her family. Beaumont remained in St. Pierre and Miquelon for a few years, until he drowned in a lake. He was found with his wooden shoes on his feet.

On Sunday morning, after breakfast, we attended prayers at the church at Eel Brook. Captain Pierre Muise officiated,[6] and he was a powerful speaker. Afterwards, we boarded a boat from Tousquet. Local girls rowed, and we landed at Jean-Louis', and he invited us

2. *There were no schools per se in Acadian villages in the early 1800s. The teachers in the townships of Clare and Argyle were outsiders for the most part and taught in the houses where they boarded. They were also often called on to prepare legal documents. Bourneuf did not give the name of the family with whom he boarded, and today, the people of Pubnico have no record of his stay in their village. Because he went to Tousquet with Joseph Belliveau, perhaps he lived with the Belliveaus.*

3. *Jean Belliveau married Thècle Surette, daughter of Jean-Louis Surette and Rosalie Amirault, on October 22, 1827. The younger Joseph was born on July 5, 1794, and never married.*

4. *Pierre Bourque, son of Jean Bourque and Marie Rose Surette, married Marguerite Amirault of Clare.*

5. *Pierre Surette, known as Pierre Riche, was the son of Pierre Surette III and Hélène Bellefontaine. He married Marguerite Amirault on November 21, 1796, and they had eleven children. After she died, he married Colombe Frontain, daughter of Julien Alexandre Frontain and Anne Muise. Pierre and Colombe did not have any children.*

6. *In the absence of the priest, Father Sigogne, a respected parishioner officiated the prayers at mass. Such a service was called a "White Mass." Pierre Muise also baptized infants and conducted marriages. The church at Eel Brook was built in 1808.*

7. *It was a common belief among Acadians that a person suffering from epilepsy or other unexplained illnesses was bewitched by persons possessing powers of the devil.*

8. *People such as this black man made a living from pretending that they could provide a cure for "bewitched" individuals. This is a good description of the Acadian belief in witchcraft, and it is the only written account of*

to stay for dinner. Then we went to see Jean Cottreau. Prayers were being held, and when we arrived, all of the people were on their knees. Suddenly, a young girl started to cry out and to gesture wildly. The women present took her to another room.

When prayers were done, we were introduced to Jean Cottreau and Pierre Hinard. Cottreau asked me where I was from, and he told me where he was from. During a conversation, my three compatriots—Jean Cottreau, Pierre Hinard, Antoine Richard—and I discovered that we were all born within a fifteen-mile radius of each other. We talked all afternoon and after supper, until two o'clock in the morning.

First, we discussed the girl who had caused the commotion during prayers. She was Pierre Hinard's daughter, and Cottreau told me that she was bewitched.[7] He had even sent for a Negro[8] from Shelburne who possessed a skill for finding out who had cast the spell. Cottreau had paid the Negro a good sum of money for his travels, and when the Negro arrived, he promised to kill whoever had bewitched the girl. The Negro had a gun and a silver coin for a bullet, and he said to Cottreau, "You are going to see that I am going to kill him. This spell has been cast by someone who has a grudge against the family. You do not know who this person is or where he lives. Maybe the person came from France. But I am going to kill him wherever he is found."

"Ah, Mr. Bourneuf," Cottreau said to me, "I got down on my knees and told the Negro not to shoot. I preferred to suffer rather than to destroy a soul, and, my dear sir, I paid him and sent him back home."

We also discussed how we had come to Nova Scotia. Pierre Hinard explained that he had left France to sail to the island of St. Dominique. On the return trip from St. Dominique, his ship was caught in a calm sea and, on coming out of it, ran aground on the coast of Labrador.

Eskimos captured the crew and killed all of them except him because, he said, he was so young and handsome. Hinard stayed with the Eskimos for six months, until one day, while on shore, he caught sight of a British brig sailing towards Nova Scotia. Hinard signalled to the brig, and some men came and got him. The ship landed in Halifax, and from there, Hinard made his way to Tousquet, where he married an Acadian girl [Rosalie Muise].

Jean Cottreau said that he was captured by the British at St. Pierre and Miquelon and brought to Halifax. He escaped from there with Antoine Richard, and they came to Cape Sable, where they married soon after. Cottreau married Marie Hinard [one of Pierre Hinard's daughters]; Richard, Cécile Doucet [of Tousquet]. When I went back to France in 1846, I visited St. Pair, the birthplace of Richard and Cottreau. Cottreau had a sister, Mrs. Desjardin, a widow with four daughters, who were well off. Cottreau was also godfather to his sister.

The following day, my two companions and I returned to Pubnico, stopping at Eel Brook on the way.

I taught at Pubnico for the remainder of the winter. In the spring of 1813, Benoni d'Entremont,[9] Justice of the Peace, came to see me. He had visited me many times before, to have me write papers for him and to ask me all kinds of questions. He hardly knew how to sign his name, but as he had been Justice of the Peace for many years, the people of Pubnico feared him as much as they feared the King of England.

This time, d'Entremont told me that he had received a letter from a Mr. White of Shelburne, asking him how he dared keep an escaped French prisoner in his district without letting the Governor know about it. The letter had scared d'Entremont, and he advised me to go to St. Mary's Bay, to see Father Sigogne.

I announced to the parents of my students that the

the time, though many stories have been passed down by word of mouth.

9. *Benoni d'Entremont, son of Jacques d'Entremont II and Marguerite Amirault, lived from 1745 to 1841. A justice of the peace wielded a great deal of power in the early 1800s. He heard legal cases and could sentence people to jail for petty offences such as non-payment of debts or taxes. He could also act as an arbitrator in disputes. People in rural communities had no other means to resolve grievances, so it was wise to stay on the good side of the Justice of the Peace.*

10. *Magistrate James Lent emigrated from New York to Shelburne after the American Revolution. An ensign in the Queen's Rangers, he moved to Tusket in 1783, and he died there in 1838. He became a magistrate for Yarmouth County in 1811.*

old magistrate had ordered me to leave. We met to discuss the situation and agreed to go and see Magistrate Lent[10] at Tusket, to get his advice and a passport. Captain Simon Amirault and Joseph Belliveau went with me. We slept at Eel Brook, and the following day, we met with Magistrate Lent, who was an honest, obliging man. He gave me a passport to go and see Father Sigogne.

To St. Mary's Bay

In 1813, St. Mary's Bay comprised the area from Weymouth, at the Sissiboo River, to Beaver River, at the Yarmouth County line. At the turn of the nineteenth century, all the settlements in the area were lumped under the name St. Mary's Bay or the name Clare. The first settlers, however, had named the villages. Church Point, for example, was at one time known as La Chicaben, meaning "where small potatoes grow." After the arrival of Father Jean-Mandé Sigogne and the construction of the first church, on the point of land jutting out into the bay, local inhabitants began referring to la pointe de l'église. It is probable as well that early settlers referred to the village of Grosses Coques as les grosses coques, after the quahogs plentiful on the sand flats there. Officially, however, when Bourneuf arrived at St. Mary's Bay, present-day names such as Church Point, Comeauville, Little Brook, and Grosses Coques did not exist, though he uses them in his autobiography.

At first, it seems surprising that Bourneuf was referred to a priest living so far away from

Pubnico. In light of the seriousness of Bourneuf's situation, however, it was no wonder, for Father Jean-Mandé Sigogne enjoyed the confidence of the government. He was the only Catholic priest in that part of the province, he was a justice of the peace, and he was friends with many British officials.

Between the Deportation of 1755 and the arrival of Sigogne in 1799, the St. Mary's Bay and Cape Sable areas had no resident priest. On his arrival, Sigogne, therefore, faced an enormous challenge. He had to revalidate numerous baptisms and marriages, establish rules for religious celebrations, and impose a strict moral code for a people that had been without spiritual guidance for more than four decades. The Acadians and other Catholics accepted without question his spiritual and temporal authority. (In 1818, he took a census of the Catholics along St. Mary's Bay and enumerated 853; there would have been about the same number in Cape Sable. These two parishes comprised all the Catholics in Yarmouth and Digby counties.) Sigogne also found that his parishioners lacked adequate places of worship. He assumed the role of architect and constructed churches at Church Point and Eel Brook and later at Meteghan and West Pubnico.

To help him draft rules and regulations for the administration of his parish at St. Mary's Bay and the proper conduct in church, Sigogne held a meeting of the men of the parish. He suggested the election of a council called the Fabrique, made up of six prominent parishioners. The Fabrique, which held its first meeting on December 1, 1799, looked after church finances and decided whether new churches should be built and where to build them.

Essentially the Fabrique's functions were similar to today's parish councils. One of the rules that it enacted for church attendance, however, would certainly not be accepted nowadays. In the early 1800s, men and boys sat on one side of the church; women and girls on the other.

Father Sigogne's sermons show that he was well educated and possessed a thorough knowledge of the scriptures and of history. He not only had a perfect command of French but also of English, as demonstrated in his letters to government officials (after being exiled from France, he spent six years in England). As the most educated person in the area, Sigogne was called on to write the wills, deeds, and letters of his parishioners. In 1810, he was appointed a justice of the peace for the Township of Clare, a position he held until his death in 1844.

Bourneuf travelled seventy-five miles to see this extraordinary man. By the time Bourneuf arrived in what was later known as Church Point, Sigogne had opened a school in his church to teach the basics of French, reading, writing, and arith-

metic. He had also begun teaching four young men French, English, mathematics, geography, history, and religion in the hope that they would enter the priesthood. They did not take up the vocation, however; instead, they became merchants, justices of the peace, surveyors, and navigators.

Bourneuf himself resumed teaching, at Grosses Coques. Beginning in 1811, each district received twenty pounds from the government to build a school, as long as the district itself contributed forty pounds towards the project. Evidently, neither Pubnico nor the villages of Clare contributed money, for there were no school buildings in either area. By 1841, however—when the government of Nova Scotia passed a law permitting the teaching of French and Gaelic on an equal footing with English—Clare had 17 schools with 422 pupils.

ON THE FIRST DAY, I reached Beaver River. I slept there, and the next morning, I had breakfast at Archange Deveau's.[1] After breakfast, I started to cross the Salmon River, but Jacques Deveau[2] ran after me and told me that it was impossible to cross the river before the tide was out. He took me to his home to await low tide. I had dinner there, and I left about one-thirty in the afternoon.

In Pubnico, I had been told to watch out for a man named Antoine Grivois,[3] as he had instigated the arrest of two French prisoners. But the very first person I met was Grivois.

As I passed his house, he saw me, then saddled his black horse and galloped to catch up to me. He asked me all kinds of questions—his tongue never stopped— and he was as ugly as sin. He accompanied me as far as Meteghan, where there was a man who owned a store that sold all sorts of merchandise, including liquor, though he did not have a licence. I entered the store and asked the proprietor, Mr. Sullivan,[4] for a glass of rum. He said that he did not have any to sell. When I told Grivois what had happened, he said that if I had let him ask for it, he would have obtained some.

It was one hour before sunset. Grivois went into the store to have a drink, and I continued up the bay. Then Grivois rejoined me. When we arrived at the house of old Justinien Comeau,[5] Grivois said, "There is in this house a smart woman, but the man is an ox." We covered two miles together, then Grivois took a side road, to go to one of his sons-in-law, Jean-Baptiste Thériault.[6] Before he departed, I asked him where the nearest inn was. He told me that there was one three miles away, at Major Comeau's.[7]

I arrived at Major Comeau's after sunset. I had supper there and spent the night. After supper, the family and I talked about many things. The Major had two grown sons—Anselme,[8] who later became a mem-

1. *Archange Deveau was born in 1787, son of Jean Deveau and Marie Maillet. He and his wife, Rosalie Doucet, lived about one hundred yards from the Salmon River.*

2. *Jacques Deveau was the first Acadian settler at Salmon River, arriving in 1786. He was born on Ile-Saint-Jean (Prince Edward Island) in 1726 and, historians say, lived to a very old age.*

3. *Antoine Grivois was really Augustin Guidry, one of the founders of St. Alphonse de Clare, between Meteghan and Mavillette. Grivois, meaning "ribald," was a long-standing nickname for the Guidry family. Augustin Guidry married Marie Johnson, daughter of William Johnson, of Annapolis Royal.*

4. *Mr. Sullivan was an Irish immigrant in Meteghan. He first kept a store, then his family operated the Meteghan-Petit Passage ferry.*

5. *Justinien Comeau, son of François Comeau and Madeleine Lord, was born in 1729 at Chipoudy, New Brunswick. In 1756, he married Natalie Bastarache. He purchased Deputy*

Provincial Surveyor John Morrison's land grant at Meteghan River.

6. *Jean-Baptiste Thériault, son of Alexis Thériault, was married to Augustin Guidry's daughter Marie Joseph.*

7. *Major François Comeau was the son of François Comeau and Félicité LeBlanc. He married Marguerite Melanson, and they had seven children. They lived in the village now known as Comeauville.*

8. *Anselme Comeau was a member of the Legislative Assembly from 1840 to 1855 and of the Legislative Council from 1855 until his death in 1867. The Legislative Council was the upper house, or senate, of the Nova Scotia government until its abolition in 1927. Members were appointed for life.*

9. *Pierre Claude Saulnier does not appear to have married Major Comeau's daughter, as there is no record of a Saulnier marrying a Comeau at this time.*

10. *"Vespers" is a Roman Catholic service held on Sunday afternoon or evening. It consists of the singing of psalms and, in Acadian parishes, ends with the Blessed Sacrament.*

ber of the Legislative Assembly and the Legislative Council, and Charles—and one grown girl, in addition to two younger boys and two younger girls. The eldest girl had a boyfriend named Pierre Claude Saulnier.[9] Nicknamed "le P'tit Pierre," his tongue never stopped. He bragged about everything, about how rich he was, how his father had left him all his property, and so forth. All the while, his girlfriend was spinning and discreetly observing him. Being a stranger, I told them about France and about other countries, and they seemed to enjoy listening to my stories.

The following day was Sunday, and I left early to go and see Father Sigogne before Mass. The priest received me politely, but as Sunday morning was a busy time for him, he begged to be excused.

When I came out of the glebe house, there were many people in front of the church. There, as everywhere else, people were curious of strangers.

I noticed a man, Jean Moore, who had been a fellow prisoner. After his discharge, he had moved to St. Mary's Bay and was now living with François Gilis, whose house was about two miles north of the church. Jean and I walked arm and arm in front of the church until the beginning of Mass. Everybody was watching us, as the custom of walking arm in arm seemed strange to them.

After Mass, Father Sigogne and I discussed my problem. He knew why I had come, because I had written to him. We talked about many things until Vespers.[10]

Following Vespers, I went to see François Gilis and his wife [Rosalie Muise], and I stayed with them for three days. Before leaving for Pubnico, on May 20, 1813, I took the Oath of Allegiance[11] to the British Crown. I also agreed to teach at Grosses Coques when my contract at Pubnico was over, in two months' time. At Grosses Coques, boarding at the home of Joseph

Joppé LeBlanc,[12] I would teach thirty children and receive three louis[13] per year.

It was with a heavy heart indeed that I left Pubnico during the summer of 1813. The women where I lived seemed sad while packing my things, as if they were looking for something they could not find. When I was

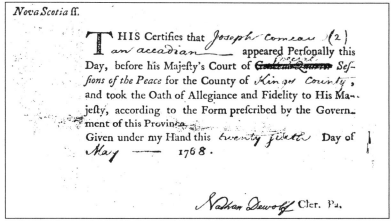

Nova Scotia ff.

THIS Certifies that *Joseph Comeau* (2) *an acadian* appeared Perſonally this Day, before his Majeſty's Court of ~~General Quarter~~ Seſſions of the Peace for the County of *Kings County*, and took the Oath of Allegiance and Fidelity to His Majeſty, according to the Form preſcribed by the Government of this Province. Given under my Hand this *twenty fifth* Day of *May* 1768.

Nathan Dewolf Cler. Pa.

ready to go, everybody in the village came to see me off. They looked at each other with tears in their eyes, and I felt as if I were leaving for my father's or my mother's funeral. Men, women, and children cried, and I wept like a baby.

Never in all my life have I regretted leaving a place more. I had found myself in Heaven, among people so sweet and affable. All Acadians are good people, but the people of Pubnico more so than others. Few days go by that I do not think of them and long for Pubnico. May God bless them.

I arrived at St. Mary's Bay with my pack on my back and almost immediately began teaching. I had one class of big boys and girls, and another of smaller children.

I abandoned teaching after one year and took up farming. François Gilis had promised to leave me his property if I lived with him and his wife. I accepted and lived with them for a long time. My foster father[14] seemed altogether pleasant.

Father Sigogne introduced the service on his arrival in St. Mary's Bay; in most Acadian parishes, it was held in the afternoon until the 1940s.

11. *In November 1764, Montague Wilmot, Governor of Nova Scotia, introduced the Oath of Allegiance to Acadians who wanted to settle in Nova Scotia and obtain land. On taking the Oath of Allegiance, a person was given a receipt such as that of Joseph Comeau.*

12. *Joseph Joppé LeBlanc and his wife, Rosalie Melanson, lived three houses from Gilis.*

13. *A "louis" was a French gold piece worth twenty francs in the early 1800s.*

14. *Bourneuf uses the term "foster father" loosely. There were no fixed rules concerning the inheritance of property in Acadian communities, as there were in France. During this period, Acadians in Nova Scotia divided their property among all their sons; often this meant that lots were subdivided to such an extent that they could*

not support a family. In cases where property was not divided, it was left to the child who would support the parents in their old age—often a daughter and her husband.

15. *Casimire LeBlanc's wife was Marie Daigle, born in Pisiquit (Windsor) before 1755.*

16. *Casimire LeBlanc was wide awake during the operation and had just eaten a hearty meal. According to witnesses, he complained only once, during the cutting of the bone. At this time, there was no such thing as anaesthetics: a tourniquet was applied above the incision, and the soft tissue was cut in such a way that it could cover the end of the bone.*

17. *The surgeon was probably Dr. George Henkell, who practised medicine in the Annapolis area from 1799 until his death in 1818.*

But I was not a good farmer. I never was, and I never will be. I was a much better fisherman. The summer of 1814, my first summer at Grosses Coques, I went fishing at Petit Passage with Joseph Joppé LeBlanc, and soon I could catch my share of fish.

One day, in the fall of 1814, Joseph Joppé LeBlanc and his wife came to the home of François Gilis. They were on their way to see a man named Casimire LeBlanc, who was going to have a leg amputated. The LeBlancs asked Mr. and Mrs. Gilis and me to accompany them. But François Gilis begged to be excused, saying that he did not feel well. So the four of us left for Church Point.

Casimire LeBlanc was eighty-four years old, and his wife[15] was almost the same age. He had broken his leg many times, and gangrene had set in. He had shown me his leg, and I had advised him to have it removed. He was a very courageous man and agreed to have it amputated,[16] but he begged me to be present during the operation. I accepted.

A surgeon from Port Royal[17] performed the amputation. The old man bled very little, as he had hardly any blood in his veins. After the operation, he became so weak that we thought he was going to die at any moment. He slowly regained his strength, however, and lived for many more years.

Casimire was born at Pisiquit, and he and his wife were taken to St. Malo at the time of the Expulsion of the Acadians. They settled in St. Servan, and during the war between England and France, Casimire enlisted with French privateers. He was captured, however, and spent a long time in a prison in England.

He became ill and was sent back to France, where he spent some time in hospital before being reunited with his wife. When the war was over, he and his wife booked passage on a fishing vessel leaving Jersey Island. The boat sailed to Arichat, on Cape Breton Island, and from

there, the LeBlancs made their way back to St. Mary's
Bay. Casimire obtained a grant of land that was right
next to the church lot.

He and his wife adopted a girl, Cécile Murat,
daughter of Pierre Murat, brother of Joachim, King of
Naples. Cécile was born in Boston, and when she was
old enough, she married Jean Melanson. They had
thirteen children, all of whom are married, except one,
who is a schoolmaster.

Joseph Joppé LeBlanc, his wife, Mrs. Gilis, and I left
Casimire LeBlanc's at midnight and returned home.
Before going in, Mrs. Gilis asked me whether it was true
that I intended to leave them. I told her that this was a
false rumour. I hardly had time to reply, however, when
François Gilis, just up from his bed, shouted angrily,
"What are you doing with my wife?" I started to grab
him by the throat, but I decided to leave and run after
Joseph LeBlanc and his wife. I quickly caught up with
them and went to their house to spend the night.

The next morning, I went to settle my accounts
with François Gilis. He asked my forgiveness and
begged me to stay with them. I agreed, on the condition that he give me an assurance in writing that I
would inherit his property on his death. He sent me to
see Father Sigogne, who would prepare the necessary

18. *When a property owner had no direct heirs, he sometimes willed his land to the local church. At Church Point, the land on which the church, the glebe house, the cemetery and the university are situated was left to the church in 1838. A large lot of land in Comeauville was left to Father Sigogne and two others in trust for a "common." And in 1818, Sigogne obtained for himself and 150 others a grant of 35,410 acres; one of the villages in this grant was appropriately named Sigogne.*

19. *Julien Blinn came to St. Mary's Bay some time between 1780 and 1785. He settled on his father-in-law's grant of 390 acres at Grosses Coques and later sold his lot to François Gilis and moved to the region of Plympton-Barton. Blinn was the first Catholic enumerated in Sigogne's 1823-1829 census. (Sigogne conducted three censuses: 1818-1822, 1823-1829, and 1840-1844.)*

20. *Gilis' adopted daughter was Elizabeth Belenfant. In 1844, Gilis' widow was living with Elizabeth and her husband.*

documents. Father Sigogne, in turn, refused to draft the papers until he spoke with Gilis.

Nothing came of it, however. Apparently, Father Sigogne had lent money to Gilis on the condition that Gilis would leave his land to him. Essentially, the priest held the land in trust,[18] as Gilis, seriously ill some time before, had drafted his will, leaving all his property to Father Sigogne, as long as the priest provided for Mrs. Gilis. In the event of her husband's death, she would go and live in the glebe house. François Gilis never told me about this. In fact, he was trying to hide it from me.

Now, Gilis had a large farm, a fine mare, two pairs of oxen, six cows, and many sheep and fowls. He lived like a prince, yet he was very frugal. He kept his house well stocked with liquor, and all passers-by visited him. Well educated, he had the respect of everyone in the community, including Father Sigogne, who called him his best friend.

Gilis had been born in France, but had lived in Eel Brook for many years. There, he met and married Rosalie Muise, daughter of Pierre Muise. They had only one child, who died very young. Father Sigogne persuaded Gilis and his wife to come and live in Grosses Coques and helped them pay for their farm, which they bought from another Frenchman[19] from the old country.

Gilis, however, paid more for the farm in Grosses Coques than he made from the sale of his farm in Eel Brook. Also, he could not sell all the land that he owned in Yarmouth County, so he left some to his adopted daughter,[20] who married [Pierre Thibault] and had a large family.

After I found out that Gilis had left his property to Sigogne, I decided to leave his home. People told me that he was jealous, but I did not believe them. I soon realized, however, that he really was jealous, even though I never gave him any reason to be.

To Sea Again

G iven that Bourneuf came from a long line of seafaring men, it is not surprising that he returned to the sea within a year of arriving at Grosses Coques. His experience served him in good stead with fishermen and with merchants who needed able seamen to man their ships.

Most of the fishing on St. Mary's Bay was done by handlining, and the principal catch was cod, pol-lock, haddock, and mackerel; herring and flat fish were trapped in weirs close to the shore. Cod and pollock were lightly salted, and dried on racks called vignaux. *After the fish was dried, it was packed in quintals (one-hundred-pound weights) and shipped to Saint John, New Brunswick, the United States, or the West Indies.*

Bourneuf found a subsistence economy on the French Shore; each family owned a large area of woodland, a small farm with fertile but rocky soil, and a small boat for inshore fishing called a bartchette. *In the following, from* Along the Shores of St. Mary's Bay, *Willie Belliveau of Belliveau Cove, born in 1889, describes Acadian life in the early 1800s:*

*Acadians of Church
Point, c. 1850:
Pierrotte Belliveau and
his family.*

In our great-grandfather's time each family in this area
got almost its entire supply of food from its small culti-
vated piece of land, from fishing either in the bay or in
the rivers and lakes, and from the wild game and wild
fruits of the forests. Each family had at least one cow,
which provided it with milk, butter, cheese [yellow,
called "big cheese," and white, or cottage cheese]. Each
family [grew] potatoes, turnips, carrots, parsnips, beets,
and artichokes. At about half a mile or more inland,
most families had an orchard. These orchards contained
not only apple trees, but most of them also had a few
pear trees and cherry trees. On the south side of most
houses were the hop vines to provide the yeast for the

bread. A few families raised wheat, but most relied on imported flour. The woodlands ... yielded blueberries, blackberries, raspberries, huckleberries, teaberries, gooseberries and herbs such as witch hazel, polypod, wintergreen, camomile, mint, horehound, tansy and bayleaf, for medicinal purposes. Maple trees ... yielded their syrup that was boiled until only the sugar remained. Cranberries grew wild and abundantly on the lowlands.... Each family kept a pig, which was fed on the refuse from the table and garden and killed in the fall. Its meat filled a barrel with salt pork. Most families also killed a steer and salted its meat. Hens provided fresh eggs and meat, while ducks and geese were also part of all but the most destitute families' backyards, and added to the fresh meat diet of the family. Nature also provided such amenities as dandelion wine and spruce beer. In the forenoon, the housewife could walk to the seashore and get a bucket of clams or mussels or a lobster or two.... Most families had a small boat ... on which they fished in the bay ... [and] their own fish weir. Most had an eel trap made of reeds, as the Indians had taught the first settlers.

The little boys would catch *poulamon* [frost fish] and small pollock on the wharves or jetties, and partridges in *yoles* [bird traps] and rabbits in snares. Smelts would be dipnetted in the spring.

Not surprisingly, commerce was not far advanced. The first merchant on the French Shore was Captain Pierre Doucet, who obtained his captain's papers in the Thirteen Colonies before returning to Nova Scotia after the Deportation. He owned a warehouse near his home at Major's Point, Belliveau Cove. By 1800, in the community now known as Comeauville, Jean-Baptiste Comeau and his sons were operating a saw mill and a grist mill, using water from a brook to generate power.

Nor was there much shipbuilding on a large scale. (Families had been building small fishing boats in their own backyards since they first settled there.) In fact, there are no records of any ships being constructed before Bourneuf built his in 1818. In 1819, according to the Reverend John Campbell in his History of the County of Yarmouth, Anthony Landers built a 250-ton schooner, Ugonia, at Salmon River. In A Geography and History of the County of Digby, though, Isaiah Wilson does maintain that a ship was built on the Sissiboo River in "about 1793."

EVEN THOUGH I HAD made up my mind to leave
François Gilis, I stayed with this jealous old man until
June 1815. Before I left, he settled our accounts, paying
me with the money he earned from selling a pair of
oxen and some other things.

I spent the summer fishing at Grand Passage[1] with
Captain Snow[2] and Mathurin Melanson.[3] We cured our
fish at Sissiboo,[4] then shipped it to Saint John. After we
sold our catch, we sailed to Granville [Annapolis
County], to return the ship to its owners. As I had no
home, however, I stayed on the ship and sailed with
Captain Simpson, a Granville merchant who had commanded British warships. In the fall of 1815, we made
several trips to Eastport, Maine.

In November, I left Captain Simpson and went to
Sissiboo to rig the schooner *Catherine*, which Campbell
and Holden[5] had constructed for the West Indian trade.
Captain Charles Doucet[6] was given command, and I
became mate. I had kept twelve quintals of fish and
loaded them on board, as we were supposed to sail to
the Leeward Islands. When the ship was ready to de-
part, however, the owners changed their minds and told

1. *Grand Passage is the
strait between Long and
Brier islands. So named by
Champlain, it separates
Westport from Freeport.*

2. *This was John W. Snow,
also a ship owner.*

3. *Born in 1794, Mathurin
Melanson was the son of
Pierre Cyriac Melanson.*

4. *Sissiboo, the name of the
river that passes through
Weymouth, is often
applied to the village of
Weymouth itself.*

*The shipyard of W. J.
Foley, Salmon River, c.
1920. Along St. Mary's
Bay, there was little
shipbuilding on a large
scale before 1818.*

5. *Colin Campbell, Sr.,
and John Holden were
two merchant-ship
owners in Weymouth.
Holden married
Marguerite Doucet,
daughter of Joseph
Doucet and Marie
Dugas.*

6. *Captain Charles
Doucet was the son of
Denis Doucet. He was
twenty-nine years old
in 1818, according to
Father Sigogne's census
of 1818-1822.*

us to sail to Windsor, Nova Scotia, to take on a shipment of gypsum[7] for New York. One of the ship's owners came with us as a supercargo, called a *courtier* in France, and I traded some fish for some plaster.

While loading the gypsum, I dropped a large piece on my foot and crushed my big toe. I wanted to go home, but the Captain and the owner would not hear of it, and they made the cook and I change places until I felt better.

We left for New York in December, but it was a long trip. We stopped for two days at Dipper Harbour to caulk the schooner, which was leaking badly. We were further delayed when we passed the lower end of Long Island and encountered a headwind and snow. The ship was then becalmed for several days in Torpenling Cove, where we spent Christmas Day. As soon as we got a fair wind, we continued on our way, but at Stonington, we met more headwinds and more snow.

We took soundings[8] and measured only six fathoms of water, but we did not see any land. After we dropped anchor, however, we spotted the shore, and a pilot noticed us and came to offer his services. The ship owner had no money to pay the pilot, so he offered him plaster or potatoes. (At Sissiboo, we had taken aboard 125 bushels of potatoes on commission for Joseph Doucet.[9]) But the pilot wanted money, so I lent the owner what I had.

The next day, there was a fair tailwind, so we raised the sails. About fifty miles from Hell Gate,[10] there was a headwind, and we had to lay to for two days. The wind then became so fierce that we had to turn around and sail to New London, where we arrived on New Year's Day, 1816.

Two or three days passed before we left for New York, the pilot on board. We passed Hell Gate a little before sunset and reached White Hall before dark. After the ship had been tied up at the wharf and it had

8. *In the early 1800s, seamen took "soundings," or tested the depth of the water, by dropping overboard a tapered lead cylinder attached to a line. They played the line until it touched bottom, then marked the line, pulled it in, and measured it.*

9. *Joseph Doucet was the son of François Doucet, a co-founder of Church Point. He was born on May 7, 1748, and married Marie Dugas. He was Charles Doucet's uncle.*

10. *Hell Gate is a channel in the East River, between Long Island and Manhattan Island, New York. Its swift currents and rough reefs were dangerous to shipping before it was widened in 1885.*

cleared customs, we opened the hatches and started to
sell the cargo. It took ten days to sell the potatoes and
the gypsum.

Meanwhile, the ship's owner had advertised that the
schooner would be ready to take on freight, but nobody
came. The Captain, therefore, discharged the crew,
though he gave us permission to remain aboard without
wages until he found some freight for the return trip.
We waited for fifteen days and finally received a cargo of
flour for Halifax.

As mate, I had to keep a record of the cargo as it
was being loaded. I checked two or three loads, then
the Captain replaced me, to save money, and sent me
down to the hold.

Soon the ship had a full cargo. I had more than four
hundred dollars, so I went ashore to buy books for my
friends, who needed them desperately. I bought sixty
dollars' worth, and I carried them on my shoulders back
to the ship.

We left for Halifax, returning through Hell Gate.
We sailed down Long Island Strait, and we hove to at a
port called Holm's Hole, where we stayed for two days.
We left there at night and passed over the Nantucket
Bank, seeing only breakers on the shore.

Passing by Georges Bank, we met a large wind and
were at a standstill for sixty hours. Once the wind
passed, we set sail for Shelburne, to disembark some
passengers. While we were off Cape Sable, the wind
shifted to the south, and we headed for the Tusket
Islands. When we entered Lobster Bay, night surprised
us, and as it was too dark to seek a harbour, we dropped
anchor in the lee of an island, which protected us from a
strong south wind.

The wind then shifted to the north, and on the ebb
tide, the ice took us, in spite of ourselves, to the open
sea. We raised the anchor as quickly as possible and set
our course for Shelburne.

When we reached Shelburne lighthouse, the wind was coming from the north, and we had to tack all day to reach the town. In fact, it took twelve hours to get from the lighthouse to the wharf. The men of Shelburne complimented us on our seamanship and said that they had never seen a ship tack that long to reach the town.

Once at the wharf, I went ashore to see all my old acquaintances, who had treated me so well while I was in jail. Everyone seemed glad to see me again.

The next day was bitterly cold. The harbour froze as far as the eye could see, so we had to stay at Shelburne for twelve hours.

The ship owner went ashore to get saws and axes to cut the ice. Meanwhile, we started to break up the ice, but we had to abandon the task, for it was too dangerous. At night, there was another wind from the north, and it was so strong that the ice took the ship two miles from town.

When the schooner neared the lighthouse, the ice was broken. We had to drop anchor, however, for the owner was still in town. The following day, the wind died down, and we went to get him. The lawyer Colin Campbell[11] also came on board, as he had booked passage to Halifax. On arriving at Halifax, the Captain went ashore to see the ship's agent, to find out where to unload. We got orders to pull up to Cunard's wharf.

It was Saturday, so we had all day Sunday to look around Halifax. On Monday, we began unloading, and we were short six or seven barrels of flour. As I had been in charge of loading, the ship's owner wanted me to pay for them. But I argued, and I never heard any more about it.

The owner bought ten hogshead of ballast[12] to get out of the harbour. I reprimanded him for this imprudence, but I could not change his mind. Our trip had

11. This Colin Campbell was a member of the Legislative Assembly from 1793 to 1818.

12. "Ballast" is heavy material such as sand or stone that is carried in the bottom of an empty ship to prevent it from capsizing.

been so long that he was very discouraged: all the profit had been absorbed.

Outside Halifax Harbour, we picked up more ballast. I was against it, but I had to obey. We sailed out with an east-northeast wind, and then we had to reel in the sails and hove to for three days. When the wind slackened, we took soundings and discovered that we were on Georges Bank. We had rolled and bobbed up and down like demons. Then the wind shifted to the southwest, and the first land we saw was Chebogue Point.

We took on more ballast and left for Sissiboo. We arrived there at low tide, so we had to drop anchor at the mouth of the river to await high tide. The owner and the Captain went ashore and sent some young men to help us go up-river. At eleven that night, we berthed at the wharf that we had left four months before.

I left the *Catherine* but had great difficulty getting my pay. I had let the Captain and the owner have several quintals of cod at twenty-two shillings, six pence a quintal and had loaned them money many times. I also asked for my wages many times, but they did not do anything about it. So I hired a horse to go and see a lawyer in Digby. Then they paid me.

In April 1817, I took command of a small schooner. I sailed to Saint John every two weeks to trade eggs, potatoes, butter, and other products for merchandise that I sold through Joseph Joppé LeBlanc and Charles à Michaud Melanson.[13] I did well all summer, and this was really the beginning of my business.

In the fall, I sold at cost a small schooner that I had bought during the summer. In the winter of 1817-18, I had wood cut to build a larger ship, which I sold the following fall for fourteen hundred dollars, four hundred dollars more than it cost me. Then I began thinking about marriage.

13. *Charles Melanson, son of Paul Melanson and Anne Comeau, was married to Madeleine Doucet.*

Romance

In Nova Scotia, Acadians followed certain rituals before marriage. During courtship, a young man was allowed to visit his girlfriend at her home on one specified night a month. He arrived at the home and sat anywhere in the kitchen, always the gathering room of Acadian households. After talking with members of the family, he would get up on some pretext—maybe for a glass of water—and move to an unoccupied seat, where his girlfriend would soon join him. This did not mean that they would be left alone: they were always under the watchful eyes of the parents. (Bundling[1] was not known among Acadians.)

Long courtships were frowned upon: the young man had to have serious intentions if he was going to visit on special nights. Formal engagements, however, were not the rule along St. Mary's Bay. There is only one listed in the archives at the Université Sainte-Anne.

The grande demande, the formal request for the girl's hand, came after the courtship. The young man arrived with a friend to ask the parents for

1. "Bundling" was practised in pioneer communities in New England. On the night that the young man visited, parents allowed an engaged couple to lie in a bed with a board between them. This allowed the couple some degree of privacy while also observing the strict moral code of the period.

permission to marry their daughter. If permission was granted, usually the case, then the young man and woman sought permission from his parents, as well as from both their godfathers.

Then they visited the parish priest to arrange for the Marriage Mass and for the "publication of the bans," a formal announcement from the pulpit still practised today. The announcement was made on three consecutive Sundays, and its purpose was to ascertain whether there was any reason why the couple should not get married, such as adultery or bigamy, as in the case of Pierre Beaumont, of Pubnico.

In close-knit and isolated communities, most families were related by blood or through marriage. On the French Shore, marriage between first cousins was never condoned, and parents stopped any such courtships right away, though there are two known instances. Marriage between second, third, and fourth cousins required a dispensation from the priest or the bishop. These unions were quite common: in the 1850s, in Salmon River, for example, thirty-one out of the first fifty marriages were with dispensation, according to the St. Vincent de Paul parish record from 1846 to 1905.

Bourneuf offers only a glimpse of his courtship of his wife, Marie Doucet. Their courtship was somewhat stormy, and it is unlikely that they observed all the formalities. For example,

2. *Most of the parish records of St. Mary's Bay burned in 1893, and therefore the exact date of Bourneuf's wedding is not available.*

Bourneuf did not have to ask Marie Doucet's father for her hand in marriage, as he had died in 1806. Although Bourneuf does not give the date in his autobiography, he must have proposed to Marie about a year after his voyage on the Catherine.[2] *Their first child, François, was born on October 10, 1819.*

WHEN I FIRST ARRIVED in Clare, in 1813, my fellow prisoner of war Jean Moore introduced me to my neighbours. It was through him that I met the widow of Amable Doucet.[3] Her husband had been dead for seven years, and he had been the only justice of the peace in Clare. The Doucets, a respectable couple, had had twelve children—two boys and ten girls. Jean Moore took me to the Doucet home, and Marie, the youngest daughter, caught my eye. At the time, I was twenty-six years old.

When I left the Doucets, I went to see Colonel Anselme Doucet,[4] the nearest neighbour. There, I met a gentleman from Paris, Pierre Bunel, who was tutoring the Colonel's children. Bunel was well educated, and he did a lot of good for the Acadians of Clare, where he lived and taught for fifty years.

I later learned Pierre Bunel's story from a distinguished officer of the French Army, Mr. Mezengo, of Brest, who had occupied a senior post at St. Pierre and Miquelon before the French Revolution. He told me that Bunel, from a good family in Paris, had been a secretary of the Governor of St. Pierre and Miquelon. One day, tempted by the Devil, he stole the Governor's gold tobacco box. Another young man was accused of the theft and was cruelly flogged. Some time afterwards, Bunel pulled the tobacco box out of his pocket. Someone noticed it and told the Governor. Bunel was apprehended, and the incriminating box was found on him. He was whipped, and expelled from St. Pierre, and never returned to France. Instead, he boarded a ship to Nova Scotia. He died at St. Mary's Bay at an advanced age but was always considered an honest man.

After I had left Colonel Doucet's, and after I had met Pierre Bunel, I returned home, to François Gilis'. Gilis asked whether I liked the Doucet girls and which one would suit me best. When I told him that I liked Marie the best, he and his wife both laughed. They said

3. Amable Doucet was born in 1737, the son of Pierre Doucet and Marie-Joseph Robichaud. In 1755, his family was deported to Massachusetts. Doucet arrived in St. Mary's Bay in 1769 and received a lot of 350 acres at Little Brook. He sold this land to buy Jean-Belonie LeBlanc's 280-acre lot at Belliveau Cove. His first wife was Marie Broussard, who died in 1774 after giving birth to a daughter. The same year, he married Marie Gaudet, who bore eleven children. In 1793, he was appointed Justice of the Peace, and Clerk for the Township of Clare.

4. Colonel Anselme Doucet was born on May 6, 1781. Son of Captain Pierre Doucet and Marie Madeleine LeBlanc, he was well educated for the time and has left 250 letters. After 1820, he commanded two militia regiments, those of the townships of Clare and Digby. In 1830, he ran as a candidate for the Legislative Assembly but withdrew before the election was over.

that she was no good and spoiled: she did only what she wanted to do. They also thought that she was much too young for me.

But these comments did not change my mind. I often went to see Miss Doucet. I was glad to see her grow in mind and body, in wisdom and all fine things. When I first saw her, she was too young to fall in love, though she had a sister[5] who had married at age fifteen.

As time passed, I did not visit Marie that often. Even though we were engaged, she had other boyfriends. I thought that this flighty behaviour was a result of her youth, and for a time, I thought that I was going to lose her.

Her actions disgusted me, and when I left to sail on the *Catherine,* in the fall of 1816, I did not say goodbye to her. I did not think that she was behaving as a fiancée should. I resolved never to speak to her or to see her again.

When the *Catherine* arrived in New York, there was a French brig taking on passengers. I went aboard to book my passage for France, then I changed my mind. I returned to the *Catherine*—and St. Mary's Bay.

5. *Rosalie Doucet married Timothé Amirault, and they had a daughter, Marie Gertrude, born on May 21, 1802.*

Postscript

François Lambert Bourneuf ends his autobiography abruptly. He married Marie Doucet in the fall of 1818. On September 29, 1859, a description of the wedding appeared in the Yarmouth Herald:

Many years ago I was invited to a French wedding. F[rançois] had been a sailor in the French navy and had been made a prisoner and confined on Melville Island near Halifax.... [He] fell in love ... with the Belle of Belliveau Cove.

After the ceremony at the chapel, the company assembled at the home of the bride. This was one of the largest houses in Clare, but it was not large enough for the company. So Colonel D[oucet], the next neighbour, gave them the use of his house also, the largest house in Clare.

Dancing commenced about 11 o'clock in the forenoon and was kept up until towards morning the next day without intermission. While feasting was going on in one house dancing did not stop in the other. The dancing was confined to one kind commonly called the French reel, performed by two couples. If I remember rightly there were three or four fiddlers so the music never stopped.

There were two or three hundred people present. They could not all take their meal at the same time. As

one set arose from the table another sat down. The eatables consisted of all kinds of flesh and fowl boiled in the same kettle with potatoes, turnips, carrots, etc.

Of course there was a liberal supply of drinkables as well as eatables, for a French wedding in those days without a full complement of these indispensables would have been *pas grandes chose.*

Well I do recollect the old colonel getting myself and a young friend, who accompanied me, into a little room by ourselves, where he treated us to some sweet Malaga, urging us to drink *pour passer le temps.* Assuring us that it could not get into our heads.

Another peculiar feature of the French wedding of those days was the manner of making love between the young folk. This was done by the gentleman and the lady getting their chairs as near together as possible and throwing a blanket or a coverlet above their heads. In this position I suppose they would say all sorts of soft things to one another until they felt inclined for another dance. After the dance they would give up the floor and resume their *tête à tête.*

The time was thus taken up in dancing, feasting, or making love. These weddings were generally kept up for two or three days with scarcely any intermission. The dancing and feasting would begin at the house of the bride and end up at that of the groom's.

Marriage during Lent is not allowed; the weddings therefore ... generally took place around the same time, in Autumn.

The parish records of St. Mary's, Church Point, reveal much about Bourneuf's life after 1817. He and Marie had seven children between 1819 and 1838:

> *François, born October 21, 1819, married Rosalie Melanson*
>
> *Ambroise, born August 19, 1821, married Charlotte Doucet*
>
> *Marie Marthe, born September 29, 1823, married Louis LeBlanc*
>
> *Volusien Remi, born September 30, 1830, died young*
>
> *Françoise Honorine, born February 24, 1832, married Placide Thimote, then Mandé Melanson*
>
> *Pierre Philippe, born May 16, 1836, married Elizabeth Melanson*
>
> *Marguerite Catherine, born November 9, 1838, married William D. Lovitt*

Nearly a year after the birth of their first child, the St. Mary's Bay area was devastated by two fires. One spread from Beaver River to Lake Doucette; the other, on September 11 or 12, from Little Brook to Grosses Coques. Father Jean-Mandé Sigogne wrote to the Bishop of Québec on October 14, 1820, describing the Great Fire of Church Point and asking for financial assistance (translation):

Approximate area devastated by the Great Fire of 1820

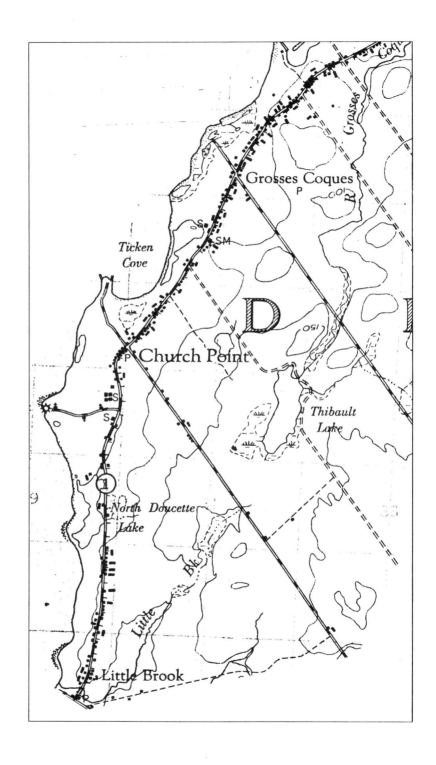

My church, my glebe, my library, my barn and other
buildings with all my property, including three quarters
of my furniture, have been burned, together with the
houses, barns, animals, fences of twenty or twenty-two
of my neighbours, all victims of a torrent of flames
driven by irresistible wind. I even found myself surrounded by the fire, which advanced faster than a gal-
loping horse. I escaped with my life but was badly
burned. I have been confined to bed and in the doctor's
care for the last thirty-two days. I have only been able
to use my right hand since two or three days. God be
praised! In our disaster, only a child in his crib and an
eighty-year-old man perished. But, alas, Your Grace,
you cannot imagine the desolation of the area and the
terrible state in which my neighbours, who were living
two miles on either side of the church, find themselves.
They are without food, without lodgings, and without
funds.

*After the fire, Bourneuf played an important role
in the restoration of the Church Point area. He
offered to rebuild the church if each family paid
him five dollars in cash or materials. Sigogne,
realizing that Bourneuf would suffer consider-
able losses, tried to increase the contributions of
parishioners, but to no avail. The church was
built in 1829, and nearly twenty-five years later,
Sigogne expressed his appreciation in a letter to
the Roman Catholic Bishop of Halifax, the Right
Reverend William Walsh:*

I owe [Bourneuf] the erection of a large and beautiful
church…. This man, a merchant, took it upon himself
to furnish all the money required to build a new church

Background: Church built in 1829 by Father Jean-Mandé Sigogne and François Lambert Bourneuf. Foreground: Ecole Apostolique des Pères Eudistes, which served as the glebe house and as a residence for priests teaching at Collège Sainte-Anne and for young men studying for the priesthood.

Ecole Apostolique des Pères Eudistes (Church-Point)   Le Collège Sainte-Anne

on condition that each family pay him five dollars in materials. This offer was accepted, and things worked out well.

Bourneuf also co-ordinated the relief of the victims. In 1859, in an appeal to the electors of Digby County, he described his efforts:

I saw so much distress that I went to the Abbe and told him if he would give me a Petition, I would go to St. John, New Brunswick, where I was well acquainted, to ask aid for the sufferers; the Abbe gave me the Petition; I owned a schooner of about 80 tons; I hired a man to take charge of her; I went to St. John in her. On landing, I went to Governor Smith, living in St. John at the time, to ask the liberty to beg for the sufferers, he gave me permission and five doubloons, this we subscribed at the head of the Petition; Henry Gilbert, Esq., subscribed £20. The Merchants held a meeting and offered their services to come with me, one each day, to go from house to house, in two weeks I had £600 subscribed. I brought £600 home and put it in a place of safety. After I was home a few days the Abbe received a

letter from Wm. A. Chipman, Esq., father of Samuel
Chipman, Esq., M.P.P., to send a schooner to get the
articles the people of Windsor, Falmouth, Horton and
Cornwallis had subscribed. As there were no vessels
besides mine, the Abbe asked me to go and I agreed. I
hired Honrble. A.F. Comeau, one Stephen LeBlanc and
Jerome Crowell, to go with me. It was late in November when we started, and the middle of December
before we returned. I delivered the whole to the Trustees—the Abbe Sigogne, C.V. Jones, Esq., and Squire
Pool from Yarmouth. The Trustees were appointed by a
Magistrate from Windsor, Falmouth, Horton, and
Cornwallis; after I delivered the articles I had nothing
more to do with them. The sufferers were very grateful
for the bread, clothes, and other necessaries of life, and
the nails and glass to rebuild their houses and barns.

*As noted in Bourneuf's appeal, he owned an 80-
ton schooner. His humble beginnings in shipbuilding, which had begun three years earlier, eventually expanded into a prosperous business. The
Bourneuf shipyard, located north of Grosses Coques and operated by Bourneuf and his sons
François, Ambroise, and Philippe, built thirty
vessels, ranging in size from 13 tons to 1,800 tons.
They included the* Balmoral *(1,200 tons), the*
Hotspur *(1,800 tons), and the* Bourneuf *(1,600
tons).*

*Bourneuf also owned timberland and operated
stores. As was the custom then in most rural areas, he paid the shipyard workers, woodcutters,
and fishermen in merchandise, not cash.*

In 1843, Bourneuf entered politics. He became a

candidate for the Reform Party, later the Liberal Party, for the Township of Digby County, which had been a separate electoral district since 1837. (In the 1837 session of the Legislative Assembly, Frederic Robichaud and Simon d'Entremont, the first Acadian representatives to the Assembly, had been instrumental in having Annapolis County divided into two counties. Thereafter, Digby County comprised three ridings. In 1843, Anselme F. Comeau was elected to represent the Township of Clare, and Bourneuf to represent the Township of Digby County. Bourneuf was an MLA for sixteen years. As the Township of Digby County was predominantly English speaking, it says a great deal about his ability and popularity, as well as the broad-mindedness of the electors.

At this time, the principal role of MLAs was to present petitions on behalf of their constituents and to act on committees. Bourneuf fulfilled this role in earnest. He sat on the legislative committees of fisheries, penitentiaries, and navigation. He also presented numerous petitions for, among others, wharves at Smith's Cove, Belliveau Cove, and Cape St. Mary's; to improve and clear the Sissiboo River channel; and for a lighthouse at the entrance to Pubnico Harbour.

In 1846, Bourneuf was appointed a justice of the peace. The following translation of the petition of the electors of Clare supporting his appointment illustrates their high regard for him:

… it is our thorough consideration that Her Majesty's justice of the peace should be if possible, a man of integrity, disinterestedness, experience and influence and above all that he should possess the confidence of the greater portion of the people.

That we are unanimous in our belief that François Bourneuf, Esq., our representative, possesses more of the above qualifications, and in a more eminent degree than any other man we know in our neighbourhood.

The year 1857 was perhaps the most eventful in Bourneuf's political career. Through his newspaper, The Novascotian, *former Liberal leader Joseph Howe launched a violent attack on Catholicism. Bourneuf and Mathurin Robichaud, together with the other Catholic Liberal members, crossed the floor of the Assembly and swelled the ranks of the Tories, bringing about the downfall of the Liberal government.*

The religious question was the central issue of the 1859 election, and the Liberals, promising to fight "Catholic ascendancy," were returned to power. This marked the end of Bourneuf's political career. Bourneuf's fortunes, in fact, had seen a sudden reversal four years earlier. In 1855, he went bankrupt. At that time, he was building an eighteen-hundred-ton vessel, the Malakoff. *Allison and Spure, shipping agents in Saint John, had agreed to purchase the schooner when it was finished. But Allison and Spure went out of business, leaving Bourneuf with a large debt. He had to declare bankruptcy in 1855. After 1855, Bourneuf, his health declining, did not play an active role in business, though he continued in politics for another four years. His shipyard was never revived, but his son François did maintain the family's retail merchandising operations.*

Bourneuf died on May 16, 1871. On June 1, the editor of the Yarmouth Herald *wrote the following: "[Bourneuf] was for a long period extensively engaged in business as a merchant, shipbuilder and shipowner. For 16 years he was a Representative of Digby County in the House of Assembly. He was a gentleman of great enterprise and usefulness and was highly esteemed."*

Appendix

*I*t seems that many of François Lambert Bourneuf's descendants followed in his footsteps, demonstrating his concern for the community and his entrepreneurial spirit.

François Bourneuf, Jr. (1819-1899)

Bourneuf's son François earned the profound respect of the community. On his death, in 1899, the historian Placide Gaudet wrote in L'Evangéline *(translation):*

François Bourneuf Jr. was born at Grosses Coques October 14, 1819, son of François Bourneuf and Marie Doucet. He was the oldest of a family of nine children. He had married Marie Rosalie Melanson on November 14, 1843, with whom he had ten children, eight of whom survive him.

The deceased was held in the highest esteem by everyone along the shores of St. Mary's Bay. He befriended the poor and was a strong supporter of education. Faithful husband and kind father, he brought up his large family to follow the principles of true Christians.

Emile Bourneuf (1884-1976)

Father Emile Bourneuf was a grandson of François Bourneuf, Jr. The son of Pierre "Pitre" Bourneuf and

Colette Comeau, he studied at Collège Sainte-Anne and at Holy Heart Seminary, in Halifax, and was ordained as a priest on June 29, 1909.

He was pastor at East Pubnico, then St. Bernard, from 1927 to 1937, and finally at Meteghan, from 1937 to 1965. While at St. Bernard, he helped continue the building of the stone church begun by the Most Reverend Alfred LeBlanc, who became Bishop of Saint John. Emile Bourneuf then watched his large brick church and glebe house perish in a fire in 1942.

In recognition of his services and his administrative abilities, Bourneuf was named Domestic Prelate while he was at St. Bernard. He retired from the ministry in 1965 and returned to the ancestral property at Grosses Coques, where he died on June 3, 1976.

Ambroise Bourneuf (1821-1903)

The second-oldest son of François Lambert Bourneuf, Ambroise, married Charlotte Doucet and worked in the family business for a time. Then he was appointed Customs Officer of the Township of Clare. The Customs Officer played an important role in the community, as stacks of documents in the archives of the Centre Acadien, Université Saint-Anne, show. Three of his grandchildren also had outstanding careers.

Ambroise Bourneuf

J. Willie Comeau (1876-1966)

J. Willie Comeau, as he was known to his constituents, was born at Comeauville on March 12, 1876, the son of Louis Pierre Comeau and Catherine Bourneuf, daughter of Ambroise.

After completing elementary school in Comeauville, he enrolled in 1890 in the first commerce course at Collège Sainte-Anne. He graduated two years later. Along with

J. Willie Comeau

his brothers Edouard and Charles, he established fishing operations at Comeauville, Arichat, Caraquet, and Moncton. Later, with his brother Gustave, he pioneered silver-fox ranching in Clare.

In 1900, he was appointed Assistant Commissioner of the Canadian pavilion at the Paris World Fair. This launched his career in public life. In 1907, he was elected an MLA for Digby County. Comeau retained his seat until 1917, when he resigned to run in the federal election on the Liberal ticket, opposed to Conscription. He was defeated but ran again provincially and won.

In 1925, he stepped down as MLA, as he was appointed to the Legislative Council. The upper house was abolished in 1927, so Comeau ran in the 1928 provincial election, which he won handily. He continued this winning streak until 1948, when he was appointed to the federal senate. He remained in the Senate until just before his death, on January 11, 1966.

During his fruitful fifty-nine-year career, he sat on many legislative committees: Private and Local Bills, Education, Human Institution, Railroads, Public Utilities, Crown Lands, Law Amendments, Contingencies, Agriculture, and Public Accounts. From 1935 to 1948, he presided over the very important committee of Rules and Privileges of the House. Between 1911 and 1917, and 1933 to 1948, he was Minister without Portfolio; during the latter period, he was also Deputy Premier.

In 1955, the Holy Father conferred on Comeau the honour of Commander of the Order of Saint Gregory the Great, and in 1961, La Société Nationale des Acadiens awarded him l'Ordre de la Fidélité Acadienne for his outstanding contribution to the advancement of Acadian culture.

Comeau's first wife was Grace Sheehan, and after her death, he married Zoé Doucet of Belliveau Cove. Six children were born from the first marriage, and eight from the second. His son Benoit followed in his footsteps, sitting in the Legislative Assembly from 1967 to 1981, and holding the Fisheries and Public Works portfolios from 1971 to 1977.

On J. Willie Comeau's death, Désiré D'Eon, editor of the West Pubnico newspaper, Petit Courrier, *wrote (translation), "The Honorable J. Willie Comeau was a man of convictions and was not afraid to voice his opinions especially when the rights of his people and his constituents were threatened. Such a long and useful career deserves our admiration."*

J. Emile LeBlanc (1890-1957)

J. Emile LeBlanc was born at Church Point, the son of Isaac LeBlanc and Aimée Bourneuf, daughter of Ambroise.

J. Emile LeBlanc

After attending the two-room Sisters of Charity school at Church Point, Emile LeBlanc took classics at Collège Sainte-Anne, obtaining his BA in 1910. He then studied medicine at Dalhousie University, in Halifax, becoming a general practitioner at West Pubnico in 1915. With dedication and compassion, he practised medicine for forty years, even while suffering ill health, which ended in his death on September 27, 1957.

Despite his strenuous medical practice, LeBlanc found time to take part in several associations that benefited Acadians. In 1919, he was elected General Counsel of the Société l'Assomption, an Acadian insurance society based in Moncton. In 1931, he became Second Vice President, a position he held until 1951. He was also a director of the Société Nationale l'Assomption, a cultural organization, until its liquidation in 1957, at which time he became one of the first directors of its successor, the Société Nationale des Acadiens. The credit-union movement, co-operative ventures, the Société du Bon Parler Français (which promoted the correct use of spoken French), and parish organizations could all rely on LeBlanc's support.

In addition, LeBlanc generously supported the Petit Courrier, *founded in 1937 by Désiré D'Eon, and, also in that year, was one of the founding members of La Bonne Presse, an association of French Catholic newspapers. For his contribution to the preservation of the French language in Acadia, the government of France awarded him the Médaille Jacques Cartier in 1934; in 1939, he received the medal of the Académie Française, and the Medal of Honor and Merit of the Société du Bon Parler Français. His alma mater conferred on him an honorary doctorate in 1954.*

LeBlanc was married to Jeannette d'Entremont of West Pubnico, daughter of Mr. and Mrs. James E. d'Entremont. They had five children: Father Maurice LeBlanc, professor of art at Université Sainte-Anne, Director of the Chorale de la Baie Sainte-Marie and of the Fanfare Régionale de Clare, and President of the Fédération Acadienne de la Nouvelle-Ecosse; Dr. Paul-Emile LeBlanc, Lyster, Québec; Roseline, retired nurse, West Pubnico; Corinne, widow of Gerald Boudreau, Wedgeport; and Simone, married to Arnold D'Eon, Melrose, Massachusetts.

Alice E. Bourneuf (1912-1980)

Ambroise Bourneuf had another famous grandchild, Alice, daughter of his son Volusien, or Wallace, as he was known in the United States. (Most of François Lambert Bourneuf's grandsons immigrated to the United States, becoming building contractors.)

Alice Bourneuf was born in Haverhill, Massachusetts. She graduated from Radcliffe in 1933, after which she became an instructor at Rosemont College, in Pennsylvania. She spent summers in Europe, doing research for her dissertation.

She was in Louvain, France, in 1940 when the Nazis invaded. She had to leave quickly, and in her haste, she lost her thesis.

During World War II, she worked for the U.S. Office of Price Administration, specializing in export-import prices. After the war, she joined the Federal Reserve Board, where she helped lay the groundwork for the International Monetary Fund. Then she was appointed to oversee the implementation of the Marshall Plan in Norway. She loved the country so much that she wrote her doctoral thesis on it: Norway, The Planned Recovery.

Eventually, Alice Bourneuf left Norway to teach at Mt. Holyoke, then at Berkeley. Finally, in 1959, she was asked to join the economics department of Boston College, a Jesuit institution; she was the first woman ever appointed to the college's Faculty of Arts and Sciences. During her eighteen-year tenure there, her department gained a national reputation. She retired from teaching in 1977 and in December 1980 died of cancer.

Bibliography

Brown, George S. *A Sequel to Campbell's History of Yarmouth County*. Boston: Rand Avery Company, 1888.

Calnek, A., and W.W. Savary. *History of the County of Annapolis*. Toronto: William Briggs, 1897.

Campbell, John R. *History of the County of Yarmouth*. Saint John, MacMillam & Co., 1876.

Clowes, Laird. *The Royal Navy: A History from the Earliest Times to the Present*. London: Sampson Low Marston & Co.

Dagnaud, P.M. *Les Français du Sud-Ouest de la Nouvelle-Ecosse*. Besançon, France: Librairie Centrale, 1905.

Deveau, J. Alphonse. *Along the Shores of St. Mary's Bay*. Church Point: Université Sainte-Anne, 1976.

Maritzs, Jean. *Artillerie de la Marine*. Paris, 1758.

Massignon, Genevieve: *Les Parlers Français d'Acadie*. Paris, 1761.

Powell, R.B. *Scrap Book of Digby Town and Municipality*. Digby, 1968.

Robertson, Marion. *King's Bounty*. Halifax: Nova Scotia Museum, 1983.

Troude, O. *Batailles Navales de la France*. Paris, 1868.

Wilson, Isaiah. *A Geography and History of the County of Digby*. Halifax: Holloway Brothers, 1900.

Miscellaneous

National Archives of Canada. *Sessional Papers*. No. 18. Ottawa, 1906.

Public Archives of Nova Scotia. *Directory of Nova Scotia M.L.A.'s*. Halifax, 1958.

———. *Place Names and Places of Nova Scotia*. Halifax, 1967.

Parish Records of St. Mary's Parish, Church Point, 1818-1822, 1823-1829, 1840-1844.

Parish Records of Cape Sable, 1899-1841 (Centre Acadien, Université Sainte-Anne, Church Point).

The Vanguard. Yarmouth, November 1970.

L'Evangéline. Weymouth, December 1891-June 1892.

Petit Courrier. West Pubnico, January 13 and 20, 1966.

Printed in Canada